Deep Learning with Hadoop

Build, implement and scale distributed deep learning models
for large-scale datasets

Dipayan Dev

BIRMINGHAM - MUMBAI

Deep Learning with Hadoop

First published: February 2017

Production reference: 1130217

Published by Packt Publishing Ltd.
Livery Place
35 Livery Street
Birmingham
B3 2PB, UK.
ISBN 978-1-78712-476-9

www.packtpub.com

Credits

Authors

Dipayan Dev

Reviewers

Shashwat Shriparv

Wissem EL Khlifi

Commissioning Editor

Amey Varangaonkar

Acquisition Editor

Divya Poojari

Content Development Editor

Sumeet Sawant

Technical Editor

Nilesh Sawakhande

Copy Editor

Safis Editing

Project Coordinator

Shweta H Birwatkar

Proofreader

Safis Editing

Indexer

Mariammal Chettiyar

Graphics

Tania Dutta

Production Coordinator

Melwyn Dsa

About the Author

Dipayan Dev has completed his M.Tech from National Institute of Technology, Silchar with a first class first and is currently working as a software professional in Bengaluru, India. He has extensive knowledge and experience in non-relational database technologies, having primarily worked with large-scale data over the last few years. His core expertise lies in Hadoop Framework. During his postgraduation, Dipayan had built an infinite scalable framework for Hadoop, called Dr. Hadoop, which got published in top-tier SCI-E indexed journal of Springer (http://link.springer.com/article/10.1631/FITEE.1500015). Dr. Hadoop has recently been cited by Goo Wikipedia in their Apache Hadoop article. Apart from that, he registers interest in a wide range of distributed system technologies, such as Redis, Apache Spark, Elasticsearch, Hive, Pig, Riak, and other NoSQL databases. Dipayan has also authored various research papers and book chapters, which are published by IEEE and top-tier Springer Journals. To know more about him, you can also visit his LinkedIn profile https://www.linkedin.com/in/dipayandev.

About the Reviewers

Shashwat Shriparv has more than 7 years of IT experience. He has worked with various technologies on his career path, such as Hadoop and subprojects, Java, .NET, and so on. He has experience in technologies such as Hadoop, HBase, Hive, Pig, Flume, Sqoop, Mongo, Cassandra, Java, C#, Linux, Scripting, PHP, C++, C, Web technologies, and various real-life use cases in BigData technologies as a developer and administrator. He likes to ride bikes, has interest in photography, and writes blogs when not working.

He has worked with companies such as CDAC, Genilok, HCL, UIDAI(Aadhaar), Pointcross; he is currently working with CenturyLink Cognilytics.

He is the author of *Learning HBase*, Packt Publishing, the reviewer of *Pig Design Pattern* book, Packt Publishing, and the reviewer of *Hadoop Real-World Solution* cookbook, 2nd edition.

I would like to take this opportunity to thank everyone who have somehow made my life better and appreciated me at my best and bared with me and supported me during my bad times.

Wissem El Khlifi is the first Oracle ACE in Spain and an Oracle Certified Professional DBA with over 12 years of IT experience. He earned the Computer Science Engineer degree from FST Tunisia, Masters in Computer Science from the UPC Barcelona, and Masters in Big Data Science from the UPC Barcelona. His area of interest include Cloud Architecture, Big Data Architecture, and Big Data Management & Analysis.

His career has included the roles of: Java analyst / programmer, Oracle Senior DBA, and big data scientist. He currently works as Senior Big Data and Cloud Architect for Schneider Electric / APC. He writes numerous articles on his website `http://www.oracle-class.com` and his twitter handle is `@orawiss`.

www.PacktPub.com

For support files and downloads related to your book, please visit www.PacktPub.com.

Did you know that Packt offers eBook versions of every book published, with PDF and ePub files available? You can upgrade to the eBook version at www.PacktPub.com and as a print book customer, you are entitled to a discount on the eBook copy. Get in touch with us at service@packtpub.com for more details.

At www.PacktPub.com, you can also read a collection of free technical articles, sign up for a range of free newsletters and receive exclusive discounts and offers on Packt books and eBooks.

https://www.packtpub.com/mapt

Get the most in-demand software skills with Mapt. Mapt gives you full access to all Packt books and video courses, as well as industry-leading tools to help you plan your personal development and advance your career.

Why subscribe?

- Fully searchable across every book published by Packt
- Copy and paste, print, and bookmark content
- On demand and accessible via a web browser

Customer Feedback

Thanks for purchasing this Packt book. At Packt, quality is at the heart of our editorial process. To help us improve, please leave us an honest review on this book's Amazon page at `https://www.amazon.com/Deep-Learning-Hadoop-Dipayan-Dev/dp/1787124762`.

If you'd like to join our team of regular reviewers, you can e-mail us at `customerreviews@packtpub.com`. We award our regular reviewers with free eBooks and videos in exchange for their valuable feedback. Help us be relentless in improving our products!

To my mother, Dipti Deb and father, Tarun Kumar Deb.

And also my elder brother, Tapojit Deb.

Table of Contents

Preface

This book will teach you how to deploy large-scale datasets in deep neural networks with Hadoop for optimal performance.

Starting with understanding what deep learning is, and what the various models associated with deep neural networks are, this book will then show you how to set up the Hadoop environment for deep learning.

What this book covers

Chapter 1, *Introduction to Deep Learning*, covers how deep learning has gained its popularity over the last decade and is now growing even faster than machine learning due to its enhanced functionalities. This chapter starts with an introduction of the real-life applications of Artificial Intelligence, the associated challenges, and how effectively Deep learning is able to address all of these. The chapter provides an in-depth explanation of deep learning by addressing some of the major machine learning problems such as, The curse of dimensionality, Vanishing gradient problem, and the likes. To get started with deep learning for the subsequent chapters, the classification of various deep learning networks is discussed in the latter part of this chapter. This chapter is primarily suitable for readers, who are interested to know the basics of deep learning without getting much into the details of individual deep neural networks.

Chapter 2, *Distributed Deep Learning for Large - Scale Data*, explains that big data and deep learning are undoubtedly the two hottest technical trends in recent days. Both of them are critically interconnected and have shown tremendous growth in the past few years. This chapter starts with how deep learning technologies can be furnished with massive amount of unstructured data to facilitate extraction of valuable hidden information out of them. Famous technological companies such as Google, Facebook, Apple, and the like are using this large-scale data in their deep learning projects to train some aggressively deep neural networks in a smarter way. Deep neural networks, however, show certain challenges while dealing with Big data. This chapter provides a detailed explanation of all these challenges. The latter part of the chapter introduces Hadoop, to discuss how deep learning models can be implemented using Hadoop's YARN and its iterative Map-reduce paradigm. The chapter further introduces Deeplearning4j, a popular open source distributed framework for deep learning and explains its various components.

Chapter 3, *Convolutional Neural Network*, introduces Convolutional neural network (CNN), a deep neural network widely used by top technological industries in their various deep learning projects. CNN comes with a vast range of applications in various fields such as image recognition, video recognition, natural language processing, and so on. Convolution, a special type of mathematical operation, is an integral component of CNN. To get started, the chapter initially discusses the concept of convolution with a real-life example. Further, an in-depth explanation of Convolutional neural network is provided by describing each component of the network. To improve the performance of the network, CNN comes with three most important parameters, namely, sparse connectivity, parameter sharing, and equivariant representation. The chapter explains all of these to get a better grip on CNN. Further, CNN also possesses few crucial hyperparameters, which help in deciding the dimension of output volume of the network. A detailed discussion along with the mathematical relationship among these hyperparameters can be found in this chapter. The latter part of the chapter focuses on distributed convolutional neural networks and shows its implementation using Hadoop and Deeplearning4j.

Chapter 4, *Recurrent Neural Network*, explains that it is a special type of neural network that can work over long sequences of vectors to produce different sequences of vectors. Recently, they have become an extremely popular choice for modeling sequences of variable length. RNN has been successfully implemented for various applications such as speech recognition, online handwritten recognition, language modeling, and the like. The chapter provides a detailed explanation of the various concepts of RNN by providing essential mathematical relations and visual representations. RNN possesses its own memory to store the output of the intermediate hidden layer. Memory is the core component of the recurrent neural network, which has been discussed in this chapter with an appropriate block diagram. Moreover, the limitations of uni-directional recurrent neural networks are provided, and to overcome the same, the concept of bidirectional recurrent neural network (BRNN) is introduced. Later, to address the problem of vanishing gradient, introduced in chapter 1, a special unit of RNN, called Long short-term Memory (LSTM) is discussed. In the end, the implementation of distributed deep recurrent neural network with Hadoop is shown with Deeplearning4j.

Chapter 5, *Restricted Boltzmann Machines*, covers both the models discussed in chapters 3 and 4 and explains that they are discriminative models. A generative model called Restricted Boltzmann machine (RBM) is discussed in chapter 5. RBM is capable of randomly producing visible data values when hidden parameters are supplied to it. The chapter starts with introducing the concept of an Energy-based model, and explains how Restricted Boltzmann machines are related to it. Furthermore, the discussion progresses towards a special type of RBM known as Convolutional Restricted Boltzmann machine, which is a combination of both Convolution and Restricted Boltzmann machines, and facilitates in the extraction of the features of high dimensional images.

Deep Belief networks (DBN), a widely used multilayer network composed of several Restricted Boltzmann machines gets introduced in the latter part of the chapter. This part also discusses how DBN can be implemented in a distributed environment using Hadoop. The implementation of RBM as well as distributed DBN using Deeplearning4j is discussed in the end of the chapter.

Chapter 6, *Autoencoders*, introduces one more generative model called autoencoder, which is generally used for dimensionality reduction, feature learning, or extraction. The chapter starts with explaining the basic concept of autoencoder and its generic block diagram. The core structure of an autoencoder is basically divided into two parts, encoder and decoder. The encoder maps the input to the hidden layer, whereas the decoder maps the hidden layer to the output layer. The primary concern of a basic autoencoder is to copy certain aspects of the input layer to the output layer. The next part of the chapter discusses a type of autoencoder called sparse autoencoder, which is based on the distributed sparse representation of the hidden layer. Going further, the concept of deep autoencoder, comprising multiple encoders and decoders is explained in-depth with an appropriate example and block diagram. As we proceed, denoising autoencoder and stacked denoising autoencoder are explained in the latter part of the chapter. In conclusion, chapter 6 also shows the implementation of stacked denoising autoencoder and deep autoencoder in Hadoop using Deeplearning4j.

Chapter 7, *Miscellaneous Deep Learning Operations using Hadoop*, focuses, mainly,on the design of three most commonly used machine learning applications in distributed environment. The chapter discusses the implementation of large-scale video processing, large-scale image processing, and natural language processing (NLP) with Hadoop. It explains how the large-scale video and image datasets can be deployed in Hadoop Distributed File System (HDFS) and processed with Map-reduce algorithm. For NLP, an in-depth explanation of the design and implementation is provided at the end of the chapter.

What you need for this book

We expect all the readers of this book to have some background on computer science. This book mainly talks on different deep neural networks, their designs and applications with Deeplearning4j. To extract the most out of the book, the readers are expected to know the basics of machine learning, linear algebra, probability theory, the concepts of distributed systems and Hadoop. For the implementation of deep neural networks with Hadoop, Deeplearning4j has been extensively used throughout this book. Following is the link for everything you need to run Deeplearning4j:

```
https://deeplearning4j.org/quickstart
```

Who this book is for

If you are a data scientist who wants to learn how to perform deep learning on Hadoop, this is the book for you. Knowledge of the basic machine learning concepts and some understanding of Hadoop is required to make the best use of this book.

Conventions

In this book, you will find a number of text styles that distinguish between different kinds of information. Here are some examples of these styles and an explanation of their meaning.

Code words in text, database table names, folder names, filenames, file extensions, pathnames, dummy URLs, user input, and Twitter handles are shown as follows: "The .build() function is used to build the layer."

A block of code is set as follows:

```
public static final String DATA_URL =
    "http://ai.stanford.edu/~amaas/data/sentiment/*";
```

When we wish to draw your attention to a particular part of a code block, the relevant lines or items are set in bold:

```
MultiLayerNetwork model = new MultiLayerNetwork(getConfiguration());
Model.init();
```

New terms and **important words** are shown in bold. Words that you see on the screen, for example, in menus or dialog boxes, appear in the text like this: "In simple words, any neural network with two or more layers (hidden) is defined as a **deep feed-forward network** or **feed-forward neural** network."

Warnings or important notes appear in a box like this.

Tips and tricks appear like this.

Reader feedback

Feedback from our readers is always welcome. Let us know what you think about this book-what you liked or disliked. Reader feedback is important for us as it helps us develop titles that you will really get the most out of. To send us general feedback, simply e-mail `feedback@packtpub.com`, and mention the book's title in the subject of your message. If there is a topic that you have expertise in and you are interested in either writing or contributing to a book, see our author guide at `www.packtpub.com/authors`.

Customer support

Now that you are the proud owner of a Packt book, we have a number of things to help you to get the most from your purchase.

Downloading the example code

You can download the example code files for this book from your account at `http://www.packtpub.com`. If you purchased this book elsewhere, you can visit `http://www.packtpub.com/support` and register to have the files e-mailed directly to you.

You can download the code files by following these steps:

1. Log in or register to our website using your e-mail address and password.
2. Hover the mouse pointer on the **SUPPORT** tab at the top.
3. Click on **Code Downloads & Errata**.
4. Enter the name of the book in the **Search** box.
5. Select the book for which you're looking to download the code files.
6. Choose from the drop-down menu where you purchased this book from.
7. Click on **Code Download**.

Once the file is downloaded, please make sure that you unzip or extract the folder using the latest version of:

- WinRAR / 7-Zip for Windows
- Zipeg / iZip / UnRarX for Mac
- 7-Zip / PeaZip for Linux

The code bundle for the book is also hosted on GitHub at `https://github.com/PacktPubl ishing/Deep-Learning-with-Hadoop`. We also have other code bundles from our rich catalog of books and videos available at `https://github.com/PacktPublishing/`. Check them out!

Downloading the color images of this book

We also provide you with a PDF file that has color images of the screenshots/diagrams used in this book. The color images will help you better understand the changes in the output. You can download this file from `https://www.packtpub.com/sites/default/files/down loads/DeepLearningwithHadoop_ColorImages.pdf`.

Errata

Although we have taken every care to ensure the accuracy of our content, mistakes do happen. If you find a mistake in one of our books-maybe a mistake in the text or the code-we would be grateful if you could report this to us. By doing so, you can save other readers from frustration and help us improve subsequent versions of this book. If you find any errata, please report them by visiting `http://www.packtpub.com/submit-errata`, selecting your book, clicking on the **Errata Submission Form** link, and entering the details of your errata. Once your errata are verified, your submission will be accepted and the errata will be uploaded to our website or added to any list of existing errata under the Errata section of that title.

To view the previously submitted errata, go to `https://www.packtpub.com/books/conten t/support`and enter the name of the book in the search field. The required information will appear under the **Errata** section.

Piracy

Piracy of copyrighted material on the Internet is an ongoing problem across all media. At Packt, we take the protection of our copyright and licenses very seriously. If you come across any illegal copies of our works in any form on the Internet, please provide us with the location address or website name immediately so that we can pursue a remedy.

Please contact us at `copyright@packtpub.com` with a link to the suspected pirated material.

We appreciate your help in protecting our authors and our ability to bring you valuable content.

Questions

If you have a problem with any aspect of this book, you can contact us
at questions@packtpub.com, and we will do our best to address the problem.

1

Introduction to Deep Learning

"By far the greatest danger of Artificial Intelligence is that people conclude too early that they understand it."

– Eliezer Yudkowsky

Ever thought, why it is often difficult to beat the computer in chess, even for the best players of the game? How Facebook is able to recognize your face amid hundreds of millions of photos? How can your mobile phone recognize your voice, and redirect the call to the correct person, from hundreds of contacts listed?

The primary goal of this book is to deal with many of those queries, and to provide detailed solutions to the readers. This book can be used for a wide range of reasons by a variety of readers, however, we wrote the book with two main target audiences in mind. One of the primary target audiences is undergraduate or graduate university students learning about deep learning and Artificial Intelligence; the second group of readers are the software engineers who already have a knowledge of big data, deep learning, and statistical modeling, but want to rapidly gain knowledge of how deep learning can be used for big data and vice versa.

This chapter will mainly try to set a foundation for the readers by providing the basic concepts, terminologies, characteristics, and the major challenges of deep learning. The chapter will also put forward the classification of different deep network algorithms, which have been widely used by researchers over the last decade. The following are the main topics that this chapter will cover:

- Getting started with deep learning
- Deep learning terminologies
- Deep learning: A revolution in Artificial Intelligence
- Classification of deep learning networks

Ever since the dawn of civilization, people have always dreamt of building artificial machines or robots which can behave and work exactly like human beings. From the Greek mythological characters to the ancient Hindu epics, there are numerous such examples, which clearly suggest people's interest and inclination towards creating and having an artificial life.

During the initial computer generations, people had always wondered if the computer could ever become as intelligent as a human being! Going forward, even in medical science, the need of automated machines has become indispensable and almost unavoidable. With this need and constant research in the same field, **Artificial Intelligence** (**AI**) has turned out to be a flourishing technology with various applications in several domains, such as image processing, video processing, and many other diagnosis tools in medical science too.

Although there are many problems that are resolved by AI systems on a daily basis, nobody knows the specific rules for how an AI system is programmed! A few of the intuitive problems are as follows:

* Google search, which does a really good job of understanding what you type or speak
* As mentioned earlier, Facebook is also somewhat good at recognizing your face, and hence, understanding your interests

Moreover, with the integration of various other fields, for example, probability, linear algebra, statistics, machine learning, deep learning, and so on, AI has already gained a huge amount of popularity in the research field over the course of time.

One of the key reasons for the early success of AI could be that it basically dealt with fundamental problems for which the computer did not require a vast amount of knowledge. For example, in 1997, IBM's Deep Blue chess-playing system was able to defeat the world champion Garry Kasparov [1]. Although this kind of achievement at that time can be considered significant, it was definitely not a burdensome task to train the computer with only the limited number of rules involved in chess! Training a system with a fixed and limited number of rules is termed as *hard-coded knowledge* of the computer. Many Artificial Intelligence projects have undergone this hard-coded knowledge about the various aspects of the world in many traditional languages. As time progresses, this hard-coded knowledge does not seem to work with systems dealing with huge amounts of data. Moreover, the number of rules that the data was following also kept changing in a frequent manner. Therefore, most of the projects following that system failed to stand up to the height of expectation.

The setbacks faced by this hard-coded knowledge implied that those artificial intelligence systems needed some way of generalizing patterns and rules from the supplied raw data, without the need for external spoon-feeding. The proficiency of a system to do so is termed as *machine learning*. There are various successful machine learning implementations which we use in our daily life. A few of the most common and important implementations are as follows:

- **Spam detection**: Given an e-mail in your inbox, the model can detect whether to put that e-mail in spam or in the inbox folder. A common naive Bayes model can distinguish between such e-mails.
- **Credit card fraud detection**: A model that can detect whether a number of transactions performed at a specific time interval are carried out by the original customer or not.
- One of the most popular machine learning models, given by Mor-Yosef et al in 1990, used logistic regression, which could recommend whether caesarean delivery was needed for the patient or not!

There are many such models which have been implemented with the help of machine learning techniques.

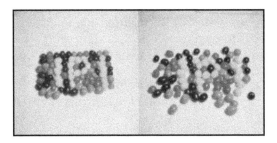

Figure 1.1: The figure shows the example of different types of representation. Let's say we want to train the machine to detect some empty spaces in between the jelly beans. In the image on the right side, we have sparse jelly beans, and it would be easier for the AI system to determine the empty parts. However, in the image on the left side, we have extremely compact jelly beans, and hence, it will be an extremely difficult task for the machine to find the empty spaces. Images sourced from USC-SIPI image database

A large portion of performance of the machine learning systems depends on the data fed to the system. This is called *representation* of the data. All the information related to the representation is called the *feature* of the data. For example, if logistic regression is used to detect a brain tumor in a patient, the AI system will not try to diagnose the patient directly! Rather, the concerned doctor will provide the necessary input to the systems according to the common symptoms of that patient. The AI system will then match those inputs with the already received past inputs which were used to train the system.

Based on the predictive analysis of the system, it will provide its decision regarding the disease. Although logistic regression can learn and decide based on the features given, it cannot influence or modify the way features are defined. Logistic regression is a type of regression model where the dependent variable has a limited number of possible values based on the independent variable, unlike linear regression. So, for example, if that model was provided with a caesarean patient's report instead of the brain tumor patient's report, it would surely fail to predict the correct outcome, as the given features would never match with the trained data.

These dependencies of the machine learning systems on the representation of the data are not really unknown to us! In fact, most of our computer theory performs better based on how the data are represented. For example, the quality of a database is considered based on how the schema is designed. The execution of any database query, even on a thousand or a million lines of data, becomes extremely fast if the table is indexed properly. Therefore, the dependency of the data representation of the AI systems should not surprise us.

There are many such examples in daily life too, where the representation of the data decides our efficiency. To locate a person amidst 20 people is obviously easier than to locate the same person in a crowd of 500 people. A visual representation of two different types of data representation is shown in the preceding *Figure 1.1*.

Therefore, if the AI systems are fed with the appropriate featured data, even the hardest problems could be resolved. However, collecting and feeding the desired data in the correct way to the system has been a serious impediment for the computer programmer.

There can be numerous real-time scenarios where extracting the features could be a cumbersome task. Therefore, the way the data are represented decides the prime factors in the intelligence of the system.

Finding cats amidst a group of humans and cats can be extremely complicated if the features are not appropriate. We know that cats have tails; therefore, we might like to detect the presence of tails as a prominent feature. However, given the different tail shapes and sizes, it is often difficult to describe exactly how a tail will look like in terms of pixel values! Moreover, tails could sometimes be confused with the hands of humans. Also, overlapping of some objects could omit the presence of a cat's tail, making the image even more complicated.

From all the above discussions, it can be concluded that the success of AI systems depends mainly on how the data are represented. Also, various representations can ensnare and cache the different explanatory factors of all the disparities behind the data.

Representation learning is one of the most popular and widely practiced learning approaches used to cope with these specific problems. Learning the representations of the next layer from the existing representation of data can be defined as representation learning. Ideally, all representation learning algorithms have this advantage of learning representations, which capture the underlying factors, a subset that might be applicable for each particular sub-task. A simple illustration is given in the following *Figure 1.2*:

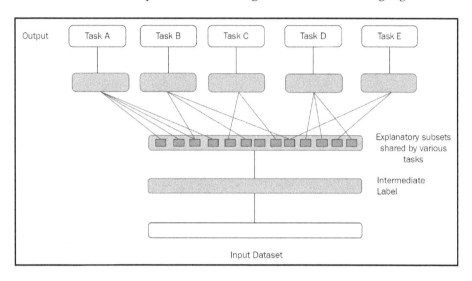

Figure 1.2: The figure illustrates representation learning. The middle layers are able to discover the explanatory factors (hidden layers, in blue rectangular boxes). Some of the factors explain each task's target, whereas some explain the inputs

However, dealing with extracting some high-level data and features from a massive amount of raw data, which requires some sort of human-level understanding, has shown its limitations. There can be many such examples:

- Differentiating the cry of two similar age babies.
- Identifying the image of a cat's eye at both day and night time. This becomes clumsy, because a cat's eyes glow at night unlike during the daytime.

In all these preceding edge cases, representation learning does not appear to behave exceptionally, and shows deterrent behavior.

Deep learning, a sub-field of machine learning, can rectify this major problem of representation learning by building multiple levels of representations or learning a hierarchy of features from a series of other simple representations and features [2] [8].

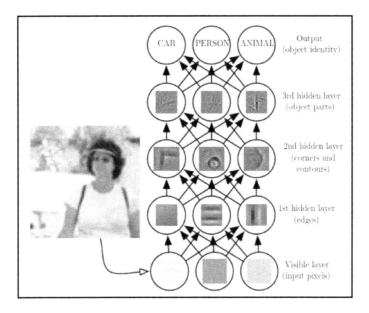

Figure 1.3: The figure shows how a deep learning system can represent the human image by identifying various combinations such as corners and contours, which can be defined in terms of edges. Image reprinted with permission from Ian Goodfellow, Yoshua Bengio, and Aaron Courville, Deep Learning, published by The MIT Press

The preceding *Figure 1.3* shows an illustration of a deep learning model. It is generally a cumbersome task for the computer to decode the meaning of raw unstructured input data, as represented by this image, as a collection of different pixel values. A mapping function, which will convert the group of pixels to identify the image, is ideally difficult to achieve. Also, to directly train the computer for these kinds of mapping is almost insuperable. For these types of tasks, deep learning resolves the difficulty by creating a series of subsets of mappings to reach the desired output. Each subset of mappings corresponds to a different set of layer of the model. The input contains the variables that one can observe, and hence , are represented in the visible layers. From the given input we can incrementally extract the abstract features of the data. As these values are not available or visible in the given data, these layers are termed as hidden layers.

In the image, from the first layer of data, the edges can easily be identified just by a comparative study of the neighboring pixels. The second hidden layer can distinguish the corners and contours from the first hidden layer's description of the edges. From this second hidden layer, which describes the corners and contours, the third hidden layer can identify the different parts of the specific objects. Ultimately, the different objects present in the image can be distinctly detected from the third layer.

Deep learning started its journey exclusively in 2006, **Hinton et al.** in 2006[2]; also **Bengio et al.** in 2007[3] initially focused on the MNIST digit classification problem. In the last few years, deep learning has seen major transitions from digits to object recognition in natural images. Apart from this, one of the major breakthroughs was achieved by **Krizhevsky et al.** in 2012 [4] using the ImageNet dataset.

The scope of this book is mainly limited to deep learning, so before diving into it directly, the necessary definitions of deep learning should be discussed.

Many researchers have defined deep learning in many ways, and hence, in the last 10 years, it has gone through many definitions too! The following are few of the widely accepted definitions:

- As noted by GitHub, deep learning is a new area of machine learning research, which has been introduced with the objective of moving machine learning closer to one of its original goals: Artificial Intelligence. Deep learning is about learning multiple levels of representation and abstraction, which help to make sense of data such as images, sounds, and texts.
- As recently updated by Wikipedia, deep learning is a branch of machine learning based on a set of algorithms that attempt to model high-level abstractions in the data by using a deep graph with multiple processing layers, composed of multiple linear and non-linear transformations.

As the definitions suggest, deep learning can also be considered as a special type of machine learning. Deep learning has achieved immense popularity in the field of data science with its ability to learn complex representation from various simple features. To have an in-depth grip on deep learning, we have listed out a few terminologies which will be frequently used in the upcoming chapters. The next topic of this chapter will help you to lay a foundation for deep learning by providing various terminologies and important networks used for deep learning.

Getting started with deep learning

To understand the journey of deep learning in this book, one must know all the terminologies and basic concepts of machine learning. However, if you already have enough insight into machine learning and related terms, you should feel free to ignore this section and jump to the next topic of this chapter. Readers who are enthusiastic about data science, and want to learn machine learning thoroughly, can follow *Machine Learning* by Tom M. Mitchell (1997) [5] and *Machine Learning: a Probabilistic Perspective* (2012) [6].

Neural networks do not perform miracles. But, used sensibly, they can produce some amazing results.

Deep feed-forward networks

Neural networks can be recurrent as well as feed-forward. Feed-forward networks do not have any loop associated in their graph, and are arranged in a set of layers. A network with many layers is said to be a deep network. In simple words, any neural network with two or more layers (hidden) is defined as a **deep feed-forward network** or **feed-forward neural network**. *Figure 1.4* shows a generic representation of a deep feed-forward neural network.

Deep feed-forward networks work on the principle that with an increase in depth, the network can also execute more sequential instructions. Instructions in sequence can offer great power, as these instructions can point to the earlier instruction.

The aim of a feed-forward network is to generalize some function f. For example, classifier $y=f(x)$ maps from input x to category y. A deep feed-forward network modified the mapping, $y=f(x; \alpha)$, and learns the value of the parameter α, which gives the most appropriate value of the function. The following *Figure 1.4* shows a simple representation of the deep-forward network, to provide the architectural difference with the traditional neural network.

A deep neural network is a feed-forward network with many hidden layers.

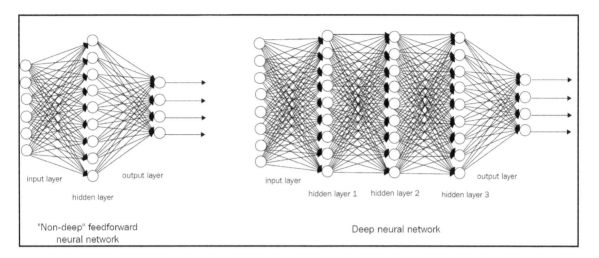

Figure 1.4: Figure shows the representation of a shallow and deep feed-forward network

Various learning algorithms

Datasets are considered to be the building blocks of a learning process. A dataset can be defined as a collection of interrelated sets of data, which is comprised of separate entities, but which can be used as a single entity depending on the use-case. The individual data elements of a dataset are called **data points**.

The following *Figure 1.5* gives the visual representation of the various data points collected from a social network analysis:

Figure 1.5: Image shows the scattered data points of social network analysis. Image sourced from Wikipedia

- **Unlabeled data**: This part of data consists of the human-generated objects, which can be easily obtained from the surroundings. Some of the examples are X-rays, log file data, news articles, speech, videos, tweets, and so on.
- **Labelled data**: Labelled data are normalized data from a set of unlabeled data. These types of data are usually well formatted, classified, tagged, and easily understandable by human beings for further processing.

From the top-level understanding, machine learning techniques can be classified as supervised and unsupervised learning, based on how their learning process is carried out.

Unsupervised learning

In unsupervised learning algorithms, there is no desired output from the given input datasets. The system learns meaningful properties and features from its experience during the analysis of the dataset. In deep learning, the system generally tries to learn from the whole probability distribution of the data points. There are various types of unsupervised learning algorithms, which perform clustering. To explain in simple words, clustering means separating the data points among clusters of similar types of data. However, with this type of learning, there is no feedback based on the final output, that is, there won't be any teacher to correct you! *Figure 1.6* shows a basic overview of unsupervised clustering:

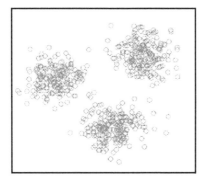

Figure 1.6: Figures shows a simple representation of unsupervised clustering

A real life example of an unsupervised clustering algorithm is Google News. When we open a topic under Google News, it shows us a number of hyper-links redirecting to several pages. Each of these topics can be considered as a cluster of hyper-links that point to independent links.

Supervised learning

In supervised learning, unlike unsupervised learning, there is an expected output associated with every step of the experience. The system is given a dataset, and it already knows how the desired output will look, along with the correct relationship between the input and output of every associated layer. This type of learning is often used for classification problems.

The following visual representation is given in *Figure 1.7*:

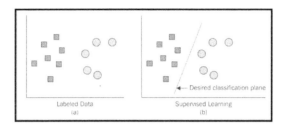

Figure 1.7: Figure shows the classification of data based on supervised learning

Real-life examples of supervised learning include face detection, face recognition, and so on.

Although supervised and unsupervised learning look like different identities, they are often connected to each other by various means. Hence, the fine line between these two learnings is often hazy to the student fraternity.

The preceding statement can be formulated with the following mathematical expression:

The general product rule of probability states that for an *n* number of datasets n ε $\mathbb{R}^t$, the joint distribution can be fragmented as follows:

$$p(n) = \sum_{i=1}^{t} p(n_i \mid n_1, n_2 \ldots, n_{i-1})$$

The distribution signifies that the appeared unsupervised problem can be resolved by *t* number of supervised problems. Apart from this, the conditional probability of *p (k | n)*, which is a supervised problem, can be solved using unsupervised learning algorithms to experience the joint distribution of *p (n, k)*.

$$p(k|n) = \frac{p(n,k)}{\sum_r p(n,r)}$$

Although these two types are not completely separate identities, they often help to classify the machine learning and deep learning algorithms based on the operations performed. In generic terms, cluster formation, identifying the density of a population based on similarity, and so on are termed as unsupervised learning, whereas structured formatted output, regression, classification, and so on are recognized as supervised learning.

Semi-supervised learning

As the name suggests, in this type of learning both labelled and unlabeled data are used during the training. It's a class of supervised learning which uses a vast amount of unlabeled data during training.

For example, semi-supervised learning is used in a Deep belief network (explained later), a type of deep network where some layers learn the structure of the data (unsupervised), whereas one layer learns how to classify the data (supervised learning).

In semi-supervised learning, unlabeled data from *p (n)* and labelled data from *p (n, k)* are used to predict the probability of *k*, given the probability of *n*, or *p (k | n)*.

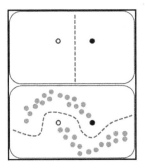

Figure 1.8: Figure shows the impact of a large amount of unlabelled data during the semi-supervised learning technique. Figure obtained from Wikipedia

In the preceding *Figure 1.8*, at the top it shows the decision boundary that the model uses after distinguishing the white and black circles. The figure at the bottom displays another decision boundary, which the model embraces. In that dataset, in addition to two different categories of circles, a collection of unlabeled data (grey circle) is also annexed. This type of training can be viewed as creating the cluster, and then marking those with the labelled data, which moves the decision boundary away from the high-density data region.

The preceding *Figure 1.8* depicts the illustration of semi-supervised learning. You can refer to *Chapelle et al.'s* book [7] to know more about semi-supervised learning methods.

So, as you have already got a foundation in what Artificial Intelligence, machine learning, and representation learning are, we can now move our entire focus to elaborate on deep learning with further description.

From the previously mentioned definitions of deep learning, two major characteristics of deep learning can be pointed out, as follows:

- A way of experiencing unsupervised and supervised learning of the feature representation through successive knowledge from subsequent abstract layers
- A model comprising of multiple abstract stages of non-linear information processing

Deep learning terminologies

- **Deep Neural Network (DNN):** This can be defined as a multilayer perceptron with many hidden layers. All the weights of the layers are fully connected to each other, and receive connections from the previous layer. The weights are initialized with either supervised or unsupervised learning.
- **Recurrent Neural Networks (RNN):** RNN is a kind of deep learning network that is specially used in learning from time series or sequential data, such as speech, video, and so on. The primary concept of RNN is that the observations from the previous state need to be retained for the next state. The recent hot topic in deep learning with RNN is **Long short-term memory (LSTM)**.
- **Deep belief network (DBN):** This type of network [9] [10] [11] can be defined as a probabilistic generative model with visible and multiple layers of latent variables (hidden). Each hidden layer possesses a statistical relationship between units in the lower layer through learning. The more the networks tend to move to higher layers, the more complex relationship becomes. This type of network can be productively trained using greedy layer-wise training, where all the hidden layers are trained one at a time in a bottom-up fashion.
- **Boltzmann machine (BM):** This can be defined as a network that is a symmetrically connected, neuron-like unit, which is capable of taking stochastic decisions about whether to remain on or off. BMs generally have a simple learning algorithm, which allows them to uncover many interesting features that represent complex regularities in the training dataset.
- **Restricted Boltzmann machine (RBM):** RBM, which is a generative stochastic Artificial Neural Network, is a special type of Boltzmann Machine. These types of networks have the capability to learn a probability distribution over a collection of datasets. An RBM consists of a layer of visible and hidden units, but with no visible-visible or hidden-hidden connections.

- **Convolutional neural networks**: Convolutional neural networks are part of neural networks; the layers are sparsely connected to each other and to the input layer. Each neuron of the subsequent layer is responsible for only a part of the input. Deep convolutional neural networks have accomplished some unmatched performance in the field of location recognition, image classification, face recognition, and so on.
- **Deep auto-encoder**: A deep auto-encoder is a type of auto-encoder that has multiple hidden layers. This type of network can be pre-trained as a stack of single-layered auto-encoders. The training process is usually difficult: first, we need to train the first hidden layer to restructure the input data, which is then used to train the next hidden layer to restructure the states of the previous hidden layer, and so on.
- **Gradient descent** (GD): This is an optimization algorithm used widely in machine learning to determine the coefficient of a function (*f*), which reduces the overall cost function. Gradient descent is mostly used when it is not possible to calculate the desired parameter analytically (for example, linear algebra), and must be found by some optimization algorithm.

In gradient descent, weights of the model are incrementally updated with every single iteration of the training dataset (epoch).

The cost function, *J (w)*, with the sum of the squared errors can be written as follows:

$$J(w) = \frac{1}{2}\sum_j((target^{(j)} - output^{(j)})^2$$

The direction of magnitude of the weight update is calculated by taking a step in the reverse direction of the cost gradient, as follows:

$$\Delta w_i = -\eta \frac{\delta J}{\delta w_i}$$

In the preceding equation, η is the learning rate of the network. Weights are updated incrementally after every epoch with the following rule:

```
for one or more epochs,
  for each weight i,
    w_i := w + Δw_i
  end
end
```

Here, $\Delta w_i = \eta \sum_j \left(\left(target^{(j)} - output^{(j)} \right) x_i^{(j)} \right)$

Popular examples that can be optimized using gradient descent are Logistic Regression and Linear Regression.

- **Stochastic Gradient Descent** (**SGD**): Various deep learning algorithms, which operated on a large amount of datasets, are based on an optimization algorithm called stochastic gradient descent. Gradient descent performs well only in the case of small datasets. However, in the case of very large-scale datasets, this approach becomes extremely costly . In gradient descent, it takes only one single step for one pass over the entire training dataset; thus, as the dataset's size tends to increase, the whole algorithm eventually slows down. The weights are updated at a very slow rate; hence, the time it takes to converge to the global cost minimum becomes protracted.

Therefore, to deal with such large-scale datasets, a variation of gradient descent called stochastic gradient descent is used. Unlike gradient descent, the weight is updated after each iteration of the training dataset, rather than at the end of the entire dataset.

```
until cost minimum is reached
  for each training sample j:
    for each weight i
      w_i := w + Δw_i
    end
  end
end
```

Here, $\Delta w_i = \eta(target^{(j)} - output^{(j)})x_i^{(j)}$

In the last few years, deep learning has gained tremendous popularity, as it has become a junction for research areas of many widely practiced subjects, such as pattern recognition, neural networks, graphical modelling, machine learning, and signal processing.

The other important reasons for this popularity can be summarized by the following points:

- In recent years, the ability of **GPU** (**Graphical Processing Units**) has increased drastically
- The size of data sizes of the dataset used for training purposes has increased significantly
- Recent research in machine learning, data science, and information processing has shown some serious advancements

Detailed descriptions of all these points will be provided in an upcoming topic in this chapter.

Deep learning: A revolution in Artificial Intelligence

An extensive history of deep learning is beyond the scope of this book. However, to get an interest in and cognizance of this subject, some basic context of the background is essential.

In the introduction, we already talked a little about how deep learning occupies a space in the perimeter of Artificial Intelligence. This section will detail more on how machine learning and deep learning are correlated or different from each other. We will also discuss how the trend has varied for these two topics in the last decade or so.

> *"Deep Learning waves have lapped at the shores of computational linguistics for several years now, but 2015 seems like the year when the full force of the tsunami hit the major Natural Language Processing (NLP) conferences."*
>
> *– Dr. Christopher D. Manning, Dec 2015*

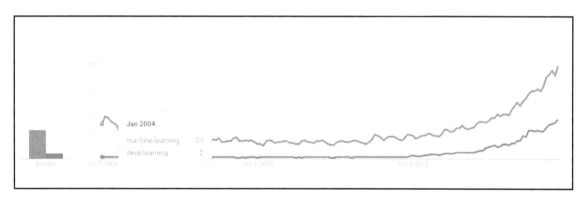

Figure 1.9: Figure depicts that deep learning was in the initial phase approximately 10 years back. However, machine learning was somewhat a trending topic in the researcher's community.

Deep learning is rapidly expanding its territory in the field of Artificial Intelligence, and continuously surprising many researchers with its astonishing empirical results. Machine learning and deep learning both represent two different schools of thought. Machine learning can be treated as the most fundamental approach for AI, where as deep learning can be considered as the new, giant era, with some added functionalities of the subject.

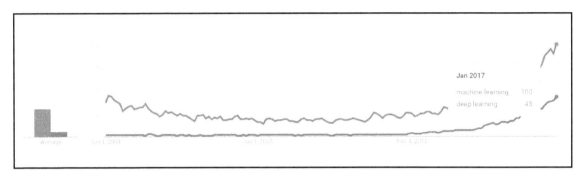

Figure 1.10: Figure depicts how deep learning is gaining in popularity these days, and trying to reach the level of machine learning

However, machine learning has often failed in completely solving many crucial problems of AI, mainly speech recognition, object recognition, and so on.

The performance of traditional algorithms seems to be more challenging while working with high-dimensional data, as the number of random variables keeps on increasing. Moreover, the procedures used to attain the generalization in traditional machine-learning approaches are not sufficient to learn complicated obligations in high-dimensional spaces, which generally impel more computational costs of the overall model. The development of deep learning was mostly motivated by the collapse of the fundamental algorithms of machine learning on such functions, and also to overcome the afore mentioned obstacles.

A large proportion of researchers and data scientists believe that, in the course of time, deep learning will occupy a major portion of Artificial Intelligence, and eventually make machine learning algorithms obsolete. To get a clear idea of this, we looked at the current Google trend of these two fields and came to the following conclusion:

- The curve of machine learning has always been the growing stage from the past decade. Deep learning is new, but growing faster than machine learning. When trends are closely observed, one will find that the growth rate is faster for deep learning compared to machine learning.

Both of the preceding *Figure 1.9* and *Figure 1.10* depict the visualizations of the Google trend.

Motivations for deep learning

One of the biggest-known problems that machine learning algorithms face is the **curse of dimensionality** [12] [13] [14]. This refers to the fact that certain learning algorithms may behave poorly when the number of dimensions in the dataset is high. In the next section, we will discuss how deep learning has given sufficient hope to this problem by introducing new features. There are many other related issues where deep architecture has shown a significant edge over traditional architectures. In this part of the chapter, we would like to introduce the more pronounced challenges as a separate topic.

The curse of dimensionality

The curse of dimensionality can be defined as the phenomena which arises during the analysis and organization of data in high-dimensional spaces (in the range of thousands or even higher dimensions). Machine learning problems face extreme difficulties when the number of dimensions in the dataset is high. High dimensional data are difficult to work with because of the following reasons:

- With the increasing number of dimensions, the number of features will tend to increase exponentially, which eventually leads to an increase in noise.
- In standard practice, we will not get a high enough number of observations to generalize the dataset.

A straightforward explanation for the curse of dimensionality could be **combinatorial explosion**. As per combinatorial explosion, with the collection of a number of variables, an enormous combination could be built. For example, with n binary variables, the number of possible combinations would be $O(2^n)$. So, in high-dimensional spaces, the total number of configurations is going to be almost uncountable, much larger than our number of examples available – most of the configurations will not have such training examples associated with them. *Figure 1.11* shows a pictorial representation of a similar phenomenon for better understanding.

Therefore, this situation is cumbersome for any machine learning model, due to the difficulty in the training. **Hughes effect** [15] states the following:

"With a fixed number of training samples, the predictive power reduces as the dimensionality increases."

Hence, the achievable precision of the model almost collapses as the number of explanatory variables increases.

To cope with this scenario, we need to increase the size of the sample dataset fed to the system to such an extent that it can compete with the scenario. However, as the complexity of data also increases, the number of dimensions almost reaches one thousand. For such cases, even a dataset with hundreds of millions of images will not be sufficient.

Deep learning, with its deeper network configuration, shows some success in partially solving this problem. This contribution is mostly attributed to the following reasons:

- Now, the researchers are able to manage the model complexity by redefining the network structure before feeding the sample for training
- Deep convolutional networks focus on the higher level features of the data rather than the fundamental level information, which extensively further reduces the dimension of features

Although deep learning networks have given some insights to deal with the curse of dimensionality, they are not yet able to completely conquer the challenge. In Microsoft's recent research on super deep neural networks, they have come up with 150 layers; as a result, the parameter space has grown even bigger. The team has explored the research with even deep networks almost reaching to 1000 layers; however, the result was not up to the mark due to *overfitting* of the model!

Over-fitting in machine learning: The phenomenon when a model is over-trained to such an extent that it gives a negative impact to its performance is termed as over-fitting of the model. This situation occurs when the model learns the random fluctuations and unwanted noise of the training datasets. The consequences of these phenomena are unsatisfactory–the model is not able to behave well with the new dataset, which negatively impacts the model's ability to generalize.

Under-fitting in machine learning: This refers to a situation when the model is neither able to perform with the current dataset nor with the new dataset. This type of model is not suitable, and shows poor performance with the dataset.

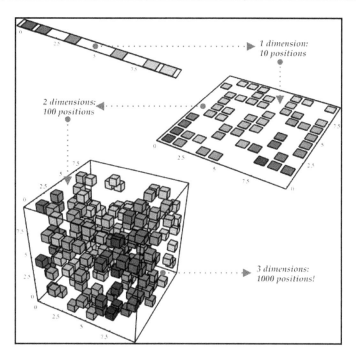

Figure 1.11: Figure shows that with the increase in the number of dimensions from one to three, from top to bottom, the number of random variables might increase exponentially. Image reproduced with permission from Nicolas Chapados from his article Data Mining Algorithms for Actuarial Ratemaking.

In the 1D example (top) of the preceding figure, as there are only 10 regions of interest, it should not be a tough task for the learning algorithm to generalize correctly. However, with the higher dimension 3D example (bottom), the model needs to keep track of all the *10*10*10=1000* regions of interest, which is much more cumbersome (or almost going to be an impossible task for the model). This can be used as the simplest example of the curse of dimensionality.

The vanishing gradient problem

The vanishing gradient problem [16] is the obstacle found while training the Artificial neural networks, which is associated with some gradient-based method, such as Backpropagation. Ideally, this difficulty makes learning and training the previous layers really hard. The situation becomes worse when the number of layers of a deep neural network increases aggressively.

The gradient descent algorithms particularly update the weights by the negative of the gradient multiplied by small scaler value (lies between 0 and 1).

$$\text{repeat until } \frac{\partial J}{\partial W_{ij}^{layer}} \to 0:$$

$$W_{ij}^{layer} := W_{ij}^{layer} - \alpha \frac{\partial J}{\partial W_{ij}^{layer}}$$

As shown in the preceding equations, we will repeat the gradient until it reaches zero. Ideally, though, we generally set some hyper-parameter for the maximum number of iterations. If the number of iterations is too high, the duration of the training will also be longer. On the other hand, if the number of iterations becomes imperceptible for some deep neural network, we will surely end up with inaccurate results.

In the vanishing gradient problem, the gradients of the network's output, with respect to the parameters of the previous layers, become extremely small. As a result, the resultant weight will not show any significant change with each iteration. Therefore, even a large change in the value of parameters for the earlier layers does not have a significant effect on the overall output. As a result of this problem, the training of the deep neural networks becomes infeasible, and the prediction of the model becomes unsatisfactory. This phenomenon is known as the vanishing gradient problem. This will result in some elongated cost function, as shown in next *Figure 1.12*:

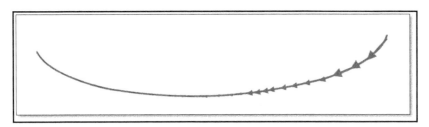

Figure 1.12: Image of a flat gradient and an elongated cost function

An example with large gradient is also shown in the following *Figure 1.13*, where the gradient descent can converge quickly:

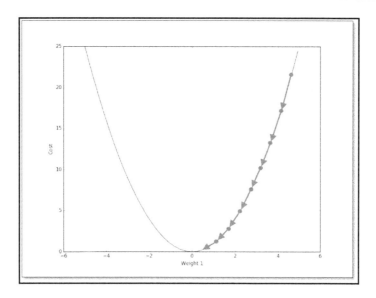

Figure 1.13: Image of a larger gradient cost function: hence the gradient descent can converge much more quickly

This is a substantial challenge in the success of deep learning, but now, thanks to various different techniques, this problem has been overcome to some extent. **Long short-term memory (LSTM)** network was one of the major breakthroughs which nullified this problem in 1997. A detailed description is given in Chapter 4, *Recurrent Neural Network*. Also, some researchers have tried to resolve the problem with different techniques, with feature preparation, activation functions, and so on.

Distributed representation

All the deep networks are mostly based on the concept of distributed representations, which is the heart of theoretical advantage behind the success of deep learning algorithms. In the context of deep learning, distributed representations are multiscale representations, and are closely related to multiscale modelling of theoretical chemistry and physics. The basic idea behind a distributed representation is that the perceived feature is the result of multiple factors, which work as a combination to produce the desired results. A daily life example could be the human brain, which uses distributed representation for disguising the objects in the surroundings.

An Artificial neural network, in this kind of representation, will be built in such a way that it will have numerous features and layers required to represent our necessary model. The model will describe the data, such as speech, video, or image, with multiple interdependent layers, where each of the layers will be responsible for describing the data at a different level of scale. In this way, the representation will be distributed across many layers, involving many scales. Hence, this kind of representation is termed as distributed representation.

A distributed representation is dense in nature. It follows a many-to-many relationship between two types of representations. One concept can be represented using more than one neuron. On the other hand, one neuron depicts more than one concept.

The traditional clustering algorithms that use non-distributed representation, such as nearest-neighbor algorithms, decision trees, or Gaussian mixtures, all require $O(N)$ parameters to distinguish $O(N)$ input regions. At one point of time, one could hardly have believed that any other algorithm could behave better than this! However, the deep networks, such as sparse coding, RBM, multi-layer neural networks, and so on, can all distinguish as many as $O(2^k)$ number of input regions with only $O(N)$ parameters (where k represents the total number of non-zero elements in sparse representation, and $k=N$ for other non-sparse RBMs and dense representations).

In these kinds of operations, either same clustering is applied on different parts of the input, or several clustering takes place in parallel. The generalization of clustering to distributed representations is termed as multi-clustering.

The exponential advantage of using distributed representation is due to the reuse of each parameter in multiple examples, which are not necessarily near to each other. For example, Restricted Boltzmann machine could be an appropriate example in this case. However, with local generalization, non-identical regions in the input space are only concerned with their own private set of parameters.

The key advantages are as follows:

- The representation of the internal structure of data is robust in terms of damage resistance and graceful degradation
- They help to generalize the concepts and relations among the data, hence enabling the reasoning abilities.

The following *Figure 1.14* represents a real-time example of distributed representations:

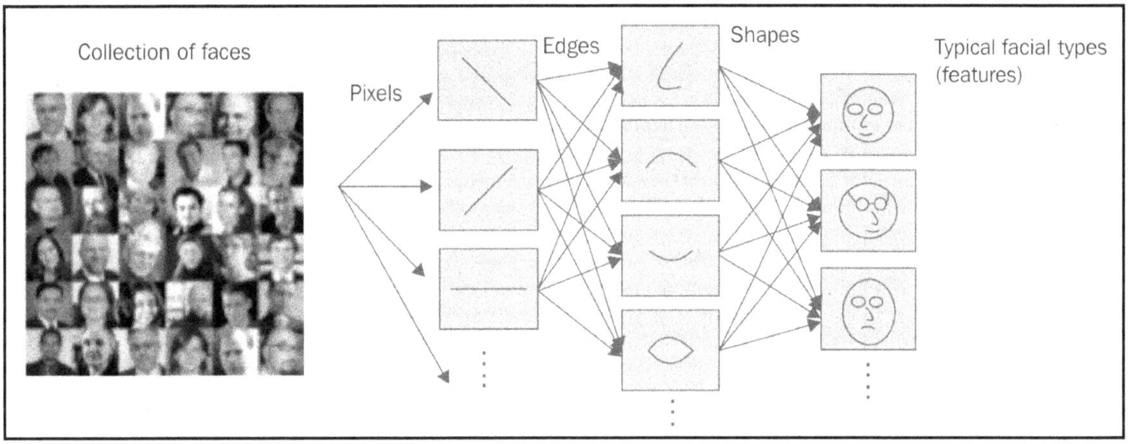

Figure 1.14: Figure shows how distributed representation helped the model to distinguish among various types of expressions in the images

Classification of deep learning networks

Artificial neural networks in machine learning are often termed as new generation neural networks by many researchers. Most of the learning algorithms that we hear about were essentially built so as to make the system learn exactly the way the biological brain learns. This is how the name **Artificial neural networks** came about! Historically, the concept of deep learning emanated from **Artificial neural networks** (**ANN**). The practice of deep learning started back in the 1960s, or possibly even earlier. With the rise of deep learning, ANN, has gained more popularity in the research field.

Multi-Layer Perceptron (**MLP**) or feed-forward neural networks with many hidden intermediate layers which are referred to as **deep neural networks** (**DNN**), are some good examples of the deep architecture model. The first popular deep architecture model was published by Ivakhnenko and Lapa in 1965 using supervised deep feed-forward multilayer perceptron [17].

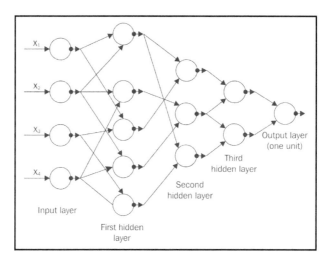

Figure 1.15: The GMDH network has four inputs (the component of the input vector x), and one output y ,which is an estimate of the true function y= f(x) = y

Another paper from Alexey Ivakhnenko, who was working at that time on a better prediction of fish population in rivers, used the **group method of data handling algorithm** (**GMDH**), which tried to explain a type of deep network with eight trained layers, in 1971. It is still considered as one of most popular papers of the current millennium[18]. The preceding *Figure 1.15* shows the GMDH network of four inputs.

Going forward, **Backpropagation** (**BP**), which was a well-known algorithm for learning the parameters of similar type of networks, found its popularity during the 1980s. However, networks having a number of hidden layers are difficult to handle due to many reasons, hence, BP failed to reach the level of expectation [8] [19]. Moreover, backpropagation learning uses the gradient descent algorithm, which is based on local gradient information, and these operations start from some random initial data points. While propagating through the increasing depth of networks, these often get collected in some undesired local optima; hence, the results generally get stuck in poor solutions.

The *optimization constraints* related to the deep architecture model were pragmatically reduced when an efficient, unsupervised learning algorithm was established in two papers [8] [20]. The two papers introduced a class of deep generative models known as a **Deep belief network** (**DBN**).

In 2006, two more unsupervised deep models with non-generative, non-probabilistic features were published, which became immensely popular with the researcher community. One is an energy-based unsupervised model [21], and the other is a variant of auto-encoder with subsequent layer training, much like the previous DBN training [3]. Both of these algorithms can be efficiently used to train a deep neural network, almost exactly like the DBN.

Since 2006, the world has seen a tremendous explosion in the research of deep learning. The subject has seen continuous exponential growth, apart from the traditional shallow machine learning techniques.

Based on the learning techniques mentioned in the previous topics of this chapter, and depending on the use case of the techniques and architectures used, deep learning networks can be broadly classified into two distinct groups.

Deep generative or unsupervised models

Many deep learning networks fall under this category, such as Restricted Boltzmann machine, Deep Belief Networks, Deep Boltzmann machine, De-noising Autoencoders, and so on. Most of these networks can be used to engender samples by sampling within the networks. However, a few other networks, for example sparse coding networks and the like, are difficult to sample, and hence, are, not generative in nature.

A popular deep unsupervised model is the **Deep Boltzmann machine (DBM)** [22] [23] [24] [25]. A traditional DBM contains many layers of hidden variables; however, the variables within the same layer have no connections between them. The traditional **Boltzmann machine (BM)**, despite having a simpler algorithm, is too much complex to study and very slow to train. In a DBM, each layer acquires higher-order complicated correlations between the responses of the latent features of the previous layers. Many real-life problems, such as object and speech recognition, which require learning complex internal representations, are much easier to solve with DBMs.

A DBM with one hidden layer is termed as a **Restricted Boltzmann machine (RBM)**. Similar to a DBM, an RBM does not have any hidden-to-hidden and visible-to-visible connections. The crucial property of an RBM is reflected in constituting many RBMs. With numerous latent layers formed, the feature activation of a previous RBM acts as the input training data for the next. This kind of architecture generates a different kind of network named **Deep belief network (DBN)**. Various applications of the Restricted Boltzmann machine and Deep belief network are discussed in detail in Chapter 5, *Restricted Boltzmann Machines*.

A primary component of DBN is a set of layers, which reduces its time complexity linear of size and depth of the networks. Along with DBN property, which could overcome the major drawback of BP by starting the training from some desired initialization data points, it has other attractive catching characteristics too. Some of them are listed as follows:

- DBN can be considered as a probabilistic generative model.
- With hundreds of millions of parameters, DBNs generally undergo the over-fitting problem. Also, the deep architecture, due to its voluminous dataset, often experiences the under-fitting problem. Both of these problems can be effectively diminished in the pre-training step.
- Effective uses of unlabeled data are practiced by DBN.

One more deep generative network, which can be used for unsupervised (as well as supervised) learning is the **sum-product network** (**SPN**) [26], [27]. SPNs are deep networks, which can be viewed as directed acyclic graphs, where the leaves of the graph are the observed variables, and the internal nodes are the sum and product operations. The 'sum' nodes represent the mixture models, and the 'product' nodes frame the feature hierarchy. SPNs are trained using the expectation-maximization algorithm together with Back propagation. The major hindrance in learning SPNs is that the gradient rapidly diminishes when moving towards the deep layers. Specifically, the standard gradient descent of the regular deep neural networks generated from the derivative of the conditional likelihood, goes through the tribulation. A solution to reduce this problem is to substitute the marginal inference with the most probable state of the latent variables, and then disseminate the gradient through this. An exceptional outcome on small-scale image recognition was presented by Domingo and Gens in [28]. The following *Figure 1.16* shows a sample SPN network for better understanding. It shows a block diagram of the sum-product network:

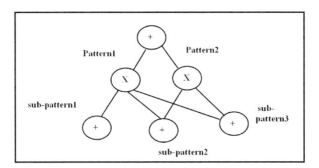

Figure 1.16: Block diagram of sum-product network

Another type of popular deep generative network, which can be used as unsupervised (as well as supervised) learning, is the **Recurrent neural network** (**RNN**). The depth of this type of network directly depends on the length of the input data sequence. In the unsupervised RNN model, experiences from previous data samples are used to predict the future data sequence. RNNs have been used as an excellent powerful model for data sequencing text or speech, however, their popularity has recently decreased due to the rise of vanishing gradient problems [29] [16]. Using stochastic curvature estimates, Hessian-free optimization [30] has somewhat overcome the limitations. Recently, Bengio et al. [31] and Sutskever [32] have come out with different variations to train the generating RNNs, which outperform the Hessian-free optimization models. RNN is further elucidated in this book in Chapter 4, *Recurrent Neural Network*.

Among the other subclasses of unsupervised deep networks, the energy-based deep models are mostly known architecture [33] [34]. A typical example of the unsupervised model category of deep networks is deep autoencoder. Most of the variants of deep autoencoder are generative in nature; however, the properties and implementations generally vary from each other. Popular examples are predictive sparse coders, Transforming Autoencoder, Denoising Autoencoder and their stacked versions, and so on. Auto-encoders are explained in detail in Chapter 6, *Autoencoders*.

Deep discriminate models

Most of the discriminative techniques used in supervised learning are shallow architectures such as Hidden Marcov models [35], [36], [37], [38], [39], [40], [41] or conditional random fields. However, recently, a deep-structured conditional random field model has evolved, by passing the output of every lower layer as the input of the higher layers. There are multiple versions of deep-structured conditional random fields which have been successfully accomplished to for natural language processing, phone recognition, language recognition, and so on. Although discriminative approaches are successful for deep-architectures, they have not been able to reach the expected outcome yet.

As mentioned in the previous section, RNNs have been used for unsupervised learning. However, RNNs can also be used as a discriminative model and trained with supervised learning. In this case, the output becomes a label sequence related to the input data sequence. Speech recognition techniques have already seen such discriminative RNNs a long time ago, but with very little success. Paper [42] shows that a Hidden Marcov Model was used to mutate the RNN classification outcome into a labelled sequence. But unfortunately, the use of Hidden Marcov model for all these reasons did not take enough advantage of the full capability of RNNs.

A few other methods and models have recently been developed for RNNs, where the fundamental idea was to consider the RNN output as some conditional distributions, and distribute all over the possible input sequences [43], [44],[45],[46]. This helped RNNs to undergo sequence classification while embedding the long-short-term-memory to its model. The major benefit was that it neither required the pre-segmentation of the training dataset, nor the post-processing of the outputs. Basically, the segmentation of the dataset is automatically performed by the algorithm, and one differentiable objective function could be derived for optimization of the conditional distributions across the label sequence. The effectiveness of this type of algorithm is extensively applicable for handwriting recognition operations.

One more popular type of discriminative deep architecture is the **convolutional neural network** (**CNN**). In CNN, each module comprises of a convolutional layer and one pooling layer. To form a deep model, the modules are generally stacked one on top of the other, or with a deep neural network on the top of it. The convolutional layer helps to share many weights, and the pooling layer segregates the output of the convolutional later, minimizing the rate of data from the previous layer. CNN has been recognized as a highly efficient model, especially for tasks like image recognition, computer vision, and so on. Recently, with specific modifications in CNN design, it has also been found equally effective in speech recognition too. **Time-delay neural network** (**TDNN**) [47] [48], originated for early speech recognition, is a special case for convolutional neural network, and can also be considered its predecessor.

In this type of model, the weight sharing is limited to only time dimension, and no pooling layer is present. `Chapter 3,` *Convolutional Neural Networks* discusses the concept and applications of CNNs in depth.

Deep learning, with its many models, has a wide range of applications too. Many of the top technology companies, such as Facebook, Microsoft, Google, Adobe, IBM, and so on are extensively using deep learning. Apart from computer science, deep learning has also provided valuable contributions to other scientific fields as well.

Modern CNNs used for object recognition have given a major insight into visual processing, which even neuroscientists can explore further. Deep learning also provides the necessary functional tools for processing large-scale data, and to make predictions in scientific fields. This field is also very successful in predicting the behaviors of molecules in order to enhance the pharmaceutical researches.

To summarize, deep learning is a sub-field of machine learning, which has seen exceptional growth in usefulness and popularity due to its much wider applicability. However, the coming years should be full of challenges and opportunities to ameliorate deep learning even further, and explore the subject for new data enthusiasts.

> To help the readers to get more insights into deep learning, here are a few other excellent and frequently updated reading lists available online:
> `http://deeplearning.net/tutorial/`
> `http://ufldl.stanford.edu/wiki/index.php/UFLDL_Tutorial`
> `http://deeplearning.net/reading-list/`

Summary

Over the past decade, we have had the privilege of hearing about the greatest inventions of deep learning from many of the great scientists and companies working in Artificial Intelligence. Deep learning is an approach to machine learning which has shown tremendous growth in its usefulness and popularity in the last few years. The reason is mostly due to its capability to work with large datasets involving high dimensional data, resolving major issues such as vanishing gradient problems, and so on, and techniques to train deeper networks. In this chapter, we have explained most of these concepts in detail, and have also classified the various algorithms of deep learning, which will be elucidated in detail in subsequent chapters.

The next chapter of this book will introduce the association of big data with deep learning. The chapter will mainly focus on how deep learning plays a major role in extracting valuable information from large-scale data.

2

Distributed Deep Learning for Large-Scale Data

"In God we trust, all others must bring data"
— W. Edwards Deming

In this exponentially growing digital world, big data and deep learning are the two hottest technical trends. Deep learning and big data are two interrelated topics in the world of data science, and in terms of technological growth, both are critically interconnected and equally significant.

Digital data and cloud storage follow a generic law, termed as Moore's law [50], which roughly states that the world's data are doubling every two years; however, the cost of storing that data decreases at approximately the same rate. This profusion of data generates more features and verities, hence, to extract all the valuable information out of it, better deep learning models should be built.

This voluminous availability of data helps to bring huge opportunities for multiple sectors. Moreover, big data, with its analytic part, has produced lots of challenges in the field of data mining, harnessing the data, and retrieving the hidden information out of it. In the field of Artificial Intelligence, deep learning algorithms provide their best output with large-scale data during the learning process. Therefore, as data are growing faster than ever before, deep learning also plays a crucial part in delivering all the big data analytic solutions.

This chapter will give an insight into how deep learning models behave with big data, and reveal the associated challenges. The later part of the chapter will introduce Deeplearning4j, an open source distributed framework, with a provision for integration with Hadoop and Spark, used to deploy deep learning for large-scale data. The chapter will provide examples to show how basic deep neural networks can be implemented with Deeplearning4j, and its integration to Apache Spark and Hadoop YARN.

The following are the important topics that will be covered in this chapter:

- Deep learning for massive amounts of data
- Challenges of deep learning for big data
- Distributed deep learning and Hadoop
- Deeplearning4j: An open source distributed framework for deep learning
- Setting up Deeplearning4j on Hadoop YARN

Deep learning for massive amounts of data

In this Exa-Byte scale era, the data are increasing at an exponential rate. This growth of data are analyzed by many organizations and researchers in various ways, and also for so many different purposes. According to the survey of **International Data Corporation** (**IDC**), the Internet is processing approximately 2 Petabytes of data every day [51]. In 2006, the size of digital data was around 0.18 ZB, whereas this volume has increased to 1.8 ZB in 2011. Up to 2015, it was expected to reach up to 10 ZB in size, and by 2020, its volume in the world will reach up to approximately 30 ZB to 35 ZB. The timeline of this data mountain is shown in *Figure 2.1*. These immense amounts of data in the digital world are formally termed as big data.

"The world of Big Data is on fire"
                                             – The Economist, Sept 2011

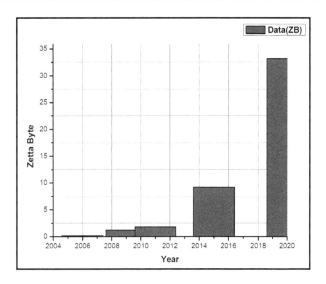

Figure 2.1: Figure shows the increasing trend of data for a time span of around 20 years

Facebook has almost 21 PB in 200M objects [52], whereas Jaguar ORNL has more than 5 PB data. These stored data are growing so rapidly that Exa-Byte scale storage systems are likely to be used by 2018 to 2020.

This explosion of data certainly poses an immediate threat to the traditional data-intensive computations, and points towards the need for some distributed and scalable storage architecture for querying and analysis of the large-scale data. A generic line of thought for big data is that raw data is extremely complex, sundry, and increasingly growing. An ideal Big dataset consists of a vast amount of unsupervised raw data, and with some negligible amount of structured/categorized data. Therefore, while processing these amounts of non-stationary structured data, the conventional data-intensive computations often fail. As a result, big data, having unrestricted diversity, requires sophisticated methods and tools, which could be implemented to extract patterns and analyze the large-scale data. The growth of big data has mostly been caused by an increasing computational processing power and the capability of the modern systems to store data at lower cost.

Considering all these features of big data, it can be broken into four distinct dimensions, often referred to as the four Vs: **Volume**, **Variety**, **Velocity**, and **Veracity**. Following *figure 2.2* shows the different characteristics of big data by providing all the 4Vs of data:

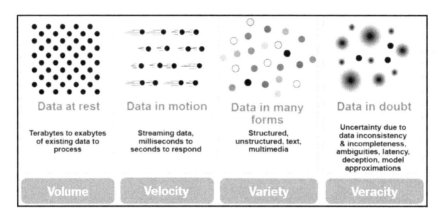

Figure 2.2: Figure depicts the visual representation of 4Vs of big data

In this current data-intensive technology era, the velocity of the data, the escalating rate at which the data are collected and obtained is as significant as the other parameters of the big data, that is, **Volume** and **Variety**. With the given pace, at which this data is getting generated, if it is not collected and analyzed sensibly, there is a huge risk of important data loss. Although, there is an option to retain this rapid-moving data into bulk storage for batch processing at a later period, the genuine importance in tackling this high velocity data lies in how quickly an organization can convert the raw data to a structured and usable format. Specifically, time-sensitive information such as flight fare, hotel fare, or some e-commerce product's price, and so on would become obsolete if the data is not immediately retained and processed in a systemic manner. The parameter veracity in big data is concerned with the accuracy of the results obtained after the data analysis. As data turns more complex each day, sustaining trust in the hidden information of big data throws a significant challenge.

To extract and analyze such critically complex data, a better, well-planned model is desired. In ideal cases, a model should perform better dealing with big data compared to data with small sizes. However, this is not always the case. Here, we will show one example to discuss more on this point.

As illustrated in *Figure 2.3*, with a small size dataset, the performance of the best algorithm is $n\%$ better than the worst one. However, as the size of the dataset increases (big data), the performance also enhances exponentially to some $k\% \gg n\%$. Such kind of traces can well be found from [53], which clearly shows the effect of a large-scale training dataset in the performance of the model. However, it would be completely misleading that with any of the simplest models, one can achieve the best performance only using Big dataset.

From [53] we can see that algorithm 1 is basically a Naive Bayes model, algorithm 2 belongs to a memory-based model, and algorithm 3 corresponds to Winnow. The following graph shows, with a small dataset, that the performance of Winnow is less that the memory-based one. Whereas when dealing with Big dataset, both the Naive Bayes and Winnow show better performance than the memory-based model. So, looking at the *Figure 2.3*, it would be really difficult to infer on what basis any one of these simple models work better in an environment of large dataset. An intuitive explanation for the relatively poor performance of the memory-based method with large datasets is that the algorithm suffered due to the latency of loading a huge amount of data to its memory. Hence, it is purely a memory related issue, and only using big data would not resolve that. Therefore, a primary reason for the performance should be how sophisticated the models are. Hence, the importance of deep learning model comes into play.

 Big data. Small Minds. No Progress! Big data. Big Brains. Breakthrough! [54]

Deep learning stands in contrast to big data. Deep learning has triumphantly been implemented in various industry products and widely practiced by various researchers by taking advantage of this large-scale digital data. Famous technological companies such as Facebook, Apple, and Google collect and analyze this voluminous amount of data on a daily basis, and have been bellicosely going forward with various deep learning related projects over the last few years.

Google deploys deep learning algorithms on the massive unstructured data collected from various sources including Google's Street view, image search engine, Google's translator, and Android's voice recognition.

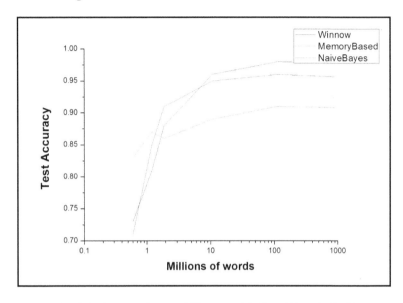

Figure 2.3: Variation of percentage of accuracy of different types of algorithms with increasing size of datasets

Apple's Siri, a virtual personal assistant for iPhones, provides a bulk of different services, such as sport news, weather reports, answers to users' questions, and so on. The entire application of Siri is based on deep learning, which collects data from different Apple services and obtains its intelligence. Other industries, mainly Microsoft and IBM, are also using deep learning as their major domain to deal with this massive amount of unstructured data. IBM's brain-like computer, Watson, and Microsoft's Bing search engine primarily use deep learning techniques to leverage the big data.

Current deep learning architectures comprise of millions or even billions of data points. Moreover, the scale at which the data is growing prevents the model from the risk of overfitting. The rapid increase in computation power too has made the training of advanced models much easier.

Table 2.1 shows how big data is practiced with popular deep learning models in recent research to get maximum information out of data:

Models	Computing power	Datasets	Average running time
Convolutional Neural Network[55]	Two NVIDIA GTX 580 3 GB GPUs.	Roughly 90 cycles through the training set of 1.2 million high resolution images.	Five to six days.
Deep Belief Network [41]	NVIDIA GTX 280 1 GB GPU.	1 million images.	Approximately one day.
Sparse autoencoder[66]	1000 CPU having 16000 cores each.	10 million 200*200 pixel images.	Approximately three days.

Table 2.1: Recent research progress of large-scale deep learning models. Partial information taken from [55]

Deep learning algorithms, with the help of a hierarchical learning approach, are basically used to extract meaningful generic representations from the input raw data. Basically, at a higher level, more complex and abstract representations of the data are learnt from the previous layers and the less abstracted data of the multi-level learning model. Although deep learning can also learn from massive amounts of labelled (categorized) data, the models generally look attractive when they can learn from unlabeled/uncategorized data [56], and hence, help in generating some meaningful patterns and representation of the big unstructured data.

While dealing with large-scale unsupervised data, deep learning algorithms can extract the generic patterns and relationships among the data points in a much better way than the shallow learning architectures. The following are a few of the major characteristics of deep learning algorithms, when trained with large-scale unlabeled data:

- From the higher level of abstractions and representation, semantics and relational knowledge of the big data can be obtained from the deep learning models
- Even a simple linear model can perform effectively with the knowledge obtained from excessively complex and more abstract representations of the huge dataset
- This huge variety of data representation from the unsupervised data opens its door for learning other data types such as textual, audio, video, image, and the like

Therefore, it can be surely concluded that deep learning will become an essential ingredient for providing big data sentiment analysis, predictive analysis, and so on, particularly with the enhanced processing power and advancement in the **graphics processing unit** (GPU) capacity. The aim of this chapter is not to extensively cover big data, but to represent the relationship between big data and deep learning. The subsequent sections will introduce the key concepts, applications, and challenges of deep learning while working with large-scale uncategorized data.

Challenges of deep learning for big data

The potential of big data is certainly noteworthy. However, to fully extract valuable information at this scale, we would require new innovations and promising algorithms to address many of these related technical problems. For example, to train the models, most of the traditional machine learning algorithms load the data in memory. But with a massive amount of data, this approach will surely not be feasible, as the system might run out of memory. To overcome all these gritty problems, and get the most out of the big data with the deep learning techniques, we will require brain storming.

Although, as discussed in the earlier section, large-scale deep learning has achieved many accomplishments in the past decade, this field is still in a growing phase. Big data is constantly raising limitations with its 4Vs. Therefore, to tackle all of those, many more advancements in the models need to take place.

Challenges of deep learning due to massive volumes of data (first V)

The volume of large-scale data imposes a great challenge to deep learning. With very high dimensionality (attributes), a large number of examples (input) and large varieties of classifications (outputs), big data often increases the complexity of the model, as well as the running-time complexity of the algorithm. The mountain of data makes the training of deep learning algorithms almost impossible using centralized storage and its limited processing ability. To provide a cushion to this challenge, pushed by the huge volume of data, distributed frameworks with parallelized servers should be used. The upgraded deep network models have started to use clusters of CPUs and GPUs to enhance the training speed, without compromising the algorithm's accuracy. Various new strategies have been evolved for model parallelism and data parallelism.

In these types, the models or data are split into blocks, which can fit with the in-memory data, and then be distributed to various nodes with forward and backward propagations [57]. Deeplearning4j, a Java-based distributed tool for deep learning, uses data parallelism for this purpose, and will be explained in the next section.

High volumes of data are always associated with noisy labels and data incompleteness. This poses a major challenge during the training of large-scale deep learning. A huge proportion of the big data is contained by the unlabeled or unstructured data, where the noisy labels predominantly exist. To overcome this issue, some manual curation of the datasets is required to a significant extent. For example, all the search engines are used to collect the data over the last one year span. For this data, we need some sort of filtering, particularly to remove redundancy and the low-value data. Advanced deep learning methods are essential to handle such noisy, redundant data. Also, the associated algorithms should be able to tolerate these disarray datasets. One can also implement some more efficient cost function and updated training strategy to fully overcome the effect of noisy labels. Moreover, the use of semi-supervised learning [58] [59] could help to enhance the solution associated with this noisy data.

Challenges of deep learning from a high variety of data (second V)

This is the second dimension of big data, which represents all types of formats, with different distributions and from numerous sources. The exponentially growing data come from heterogeneous sources, which include a mammoth collection of audio streams, images, videos, animations, graphics, and unstructured texts from various log files. These varieties of data possess different characteristics and behavior. Data integration could be the only way to deal with such situations. As stated in `Chapter 1`, *Introduction to Deep Learning*, deep learning has the ability to represent learning from structured/unstructured data. Deep learning can carry out unsupervised learning in a hierarchical fashion, which is training performed one level at a time, and the higher level features are defined by the immediate lower levels. This property of deep learning can be used to address the data integration problem. The natural solution of this could be to learn the data representation from each individual data sources, and then integrate the learned features at the subsequent levels.

There have already been a few experiments [60] [61], which have successfully demonstrated that deep learning can easily be used for the heterogeneous data sources for its significant gains in system performance. However, there are still many unanswered questions which deep learning has to address in the upcoming years. Currently, most of the deep learning models are mainly tested on bi-modalities (data from only two sources), but will the system performance be enhanced while dealing with multiple modalities? It might happen that multiple sources of data will offer conflicting information; in those cases, how will the model be able to nullify such conflicts and integrate the data in a constructive and fruitful way? Deep learning seems perfectly appropriate for the integration of various sources of data with multiple modalities, on account of its capability of learning intermediate representations and the underlying factors associated with a variety of data.

Challenges of deep learning from a high velocity of data (third V)

The extreme velocity at which data is growing poses an enormous challenge to the deep learning technique. For data analytics, data created at this speed should also be processed in a timely manner. Online learning is one of the solutions to learning from this high velocity data [62-65]. However, online learning uses a sequential learning strategy, where the entire dataset should be kept in-memory, which becomes extremely difficult for traditional machines. Although the conventional neural network has been modified for online learning [67-71], there is still so much scope for progress in this field for deep learning. As an alternate approach to online learning, the stochastic gradient descent approach [72], [73] is also applied for deep learning. In this type, one training example with the known label is fed to the next label to update the model parameters. Further, to speed up learning, the updates can also be performed on a small batch basis [74]. This mini batch can provide a good balance between running time and the computer memory. In the next section, we will explain why mini batch data is most important for distributed deep learning.

One more big challenge related to this high velocity of data is that this data is extremely changeable in nature. The distribution of data happens too frequently over time. Ideally, the data that changes over time is split into chunks taken from small time durations. The basic idea is that the data remains stationary for some time, and also possesses some major degree of correlation [75] [76]. Therefore, the deep learning algorithms of big data should have the feature of learning the data as a stream. Algorithms which can learn from those non-stationary data are really crucial for deep learning.

Challenges of deep learning to maintain the veracity of data (fourth V)

Data veracity, imprecise, or uncertain data, is sometime overlooked, though it is equally consequential as the other 3Vs of big data. With the immense variety and velocity of big data, an organization can no longer rely on the traditional models to measure the accuracy of data. Unstructured data, by definition, contains a huge amount of imprecise and uncertain data. For example, social media data is excessively uncertain in nature. Although there are tools that can automate the normalization and cleansing of data, they are mostly in the pre-industrial stage.

Distributed deep learning and Hadoop

From the earlier sections of this chapter, we already have enough insights on why and how the relationship of deep learning and big data can bring major changes to the research community. Also, a centralized system is not going to help this relationship substantially with the course of time. Hence, distribution of the deep learning network across multiple servers has become the primary goal of the current deep learning practitioners. However, dealing with big data in a distributed environment is always associated with several challenges. Most of those are explained in-depth in the previous section. These include dealing with higher dimensional data, data with too many features, amount of memory available to store, processing the massive Big datasets, and so on. Moreover, Big datasets have a high computational resource demand on CPU and memory time. So, the reduction of processing time has become an extremely significant criterion. The following are the central and primary challenges in distributed deep learning:

- How can we keep chunks of dataset in the primary memory of the nodes?
- How can we maintain coordination among the chunks of data, so that later they can be moved together to result in the final outcome?
- How can we make distributed and parallel processing extremely scheduled and coordinated?
- How can we achieve an orchestral search process across the dataset to achieve high performance?

There are multiple ways of using distributed deep learning with big datasets. However, when we talk about big data, the framework that is performing tremendously well in defending most of the challenges from the past half decade is the Hadoop framework [77-80]. Hadoop allows for parallel and distributed processing. It is undoubtedly the most popular and widely used framework, and it can store and process the data mountain more efficiently compared to the other traditional frameworks. Almost all the major technology companies, such as Google, Facebook, and so on use Hadoop to deploy and process their data in a sophisticated fashion. Most of the software designed at Google, which requires the use of an ocean of data, uses Hadoop. The primary advantage of Hadoop is the way it stores and processes enormous amount of data across thousands of commodity servers, bringing some well-organized results [81]. From our general understanding of deep learning, we can relate that deep learning surely needs that sort of distributed computing power to produce some wondrous outcomes from the input data. The Big dataset can be split into chunks and distributed across multiple commodity hardware for parallel training. Further more, the complete stage of a deep neural network can be split into subtasks, and then those subtasks can be processed in parallel.

 Hadoop has turned out to be the point of convergence for all the data lakes. The need to shif deep learning to the data, which is already residing in Hadoop, has become quintessential.

Hadoop operates on the concept that *moving computation is cheaper than moving data* [86] [87]. Hadoop allows for the distributed processing of large-scale datasets across clusters of commodity servers. It also provides efficient load balancing, has a very high degree of fault tolerance, and is highly horizontally scalable with minimal effort. It can detect and tolerate failures in the application layers, and hence, is suitable for running on commodity hardware. To achieve the high availability of data, Hadoop, by default, keeps a replication factor of three, with a copy of each block placed on two other separate machines. So, if a node fails, the recovery can be done instantly from the other two nodes. The replication factor of Hadoop can be easily increased based on how valuable the data is and other associated requirements on the data.

Hadoop was initially built mainly for processing the batch tasks, so it is mostly suitable for deep learning networks, where the main task is to find the classification of large-scale data. The selection of features to learn how to classify the data is mainly done on a large batch of datasets.

Hadoop is extremely configurable, and can easily be optimized as per the user's requirements. For example, if a user wants to keep more replicas of the data for better reliability, he can increase the replication factor. However, an increase in the number of replicas will eventually increase the storage requirements. Here we will not be explaining more about the features and configuration of data, rather we will mostly discuss the part of Hadoop which will be used extensively in distributed deep neural networks.

In the new version of Hadoop, the parts which we will mainly use in this book are HDFS, Map-Reduce, and **Yet Another Resource Negotiator** (**YARN**). YARN has already dominated Hadoop's Map-Reduce (explained in the next part) in a large manner. YARN currently has the responsibility to assign the works to the Data nodes (data server) of Hadoop. **Hadoop Distributed File System** (**HDFS**), on the other hand, is a distributed file system, which is distributed across all the Data nodes under a centralized meta-data server called NameNode. To achieve high-availability, in the later version, a secondary NameNode was integrated to Hadoop framework, the purpose of which is to have a copy of the metadata from primary NameNode after certain checkpoints.

Map-Reduce

The Map-Reduce paradigm [83] is a distributed programming model developed by Google in 2004, and is associated with processing huge datasets with a parallel and distributed algorithm on a cluster of machines. The entire Map-Reduce application is useful with large-scale datasets. Basically, it has two primary components, one is called Map and the other is called Reduce, along with a few intermediate stages like shuffling, sorting and partitioning. In the map phase, the large input job is broken down into smaller ones, and each of the jobs is distributed to different cores. The operation(s) are then carried out on every small job placed on those machines. The Reduce phase accommodates all the scattered and transformed output into one single dataset.

Explaining the concept of Map-Reduce in detail is beyond the scope of this chapter; interested readers can go through *"Map-Reduce: Simplified data processing on large clusters"* [83] to get an in-depth knowledge of this.

Iterative Map-Reduce

The deep learning algorithms are iterative in nature – the models learn from the optimization algorithms, which go through multiple steps so that it leads to a point of minimal error. For these kinds of models the Map-Reduce application does not seem to work as efficiently as it does for other use-cases.

Iterative Map-Reduce, a next generation YARN framework (unlike the traditional Map-Reduce) does multiple iterations on the data, which passes through only once. Although the architecture of Iterative Map-Reduce and Map-Reduce is dissimilar in design, the high level of understanding of both the architectures is simple. Iterative Map-Reduce is nothing but a sequence of Map-Reduce operations, where the output of the first Map-Reduce operation becomes the input to the next operation and so on. In the case of deep learning models, the map phase places all the operations of a particular iteration on each node of the distributed systems. It then distributes that massive input dataset to all the machines in the cluster. The training of the models is performed on each node of the cluster.

Before sending the aggregated new model back to each of the machines, the reduce phase takes all the outputs collected from the map phase and calculates the average of the parameters. The same operations are iterated over and over again by the Iterative Reduce algorithm until the learning process completes and the errors minimize to almost zero.

Figure 2.4 compares the high-level functionalities of the two methods. The left image shows the block diagram of Map-Reduce, while on the right, we have the close-up of Iterative Map-Reduce. Each 'Processor' is a working deep network, which is learning on small chunks of the larger dataset. In the 'Superstep' phase, the averaging of the parameters is done before the entire model is redistributed to the whole cluster as shown in the following diagram:

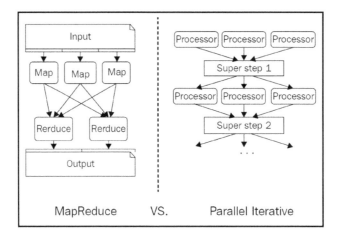

Figure 2.4: Difference of functionalities in Map-Reduce and parallel iterative reduce

Yet Another Resource Negotiator (YARN)

The primary idea of YARN is to dissociate job scheduling and resource management from the data processing. So the data can continue to process in the system in parallel with the Map-Reduce batch jobs. YARN possesses a central resource manager, which mostly manages the Hadoop system resources according to the need. The node manager (specific to nodes) is responsible for managing and monitoring the processing of individual nodes of the cluster. This processing is dedicatedly controlled by an ApplicationMaster, which monitors the resources from the central resource manager, and works with the node manager to monitor and execute the tasks. The following figure gives an overview of the architecture of YARN:

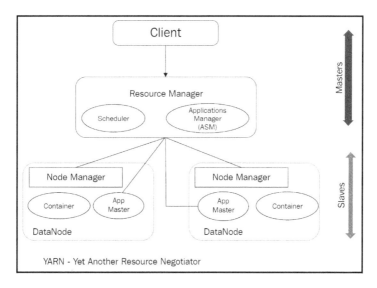

Figure 2.5: An overview of the high-level architecture of YARN

All these components of Hadoop are primarily used in distributed deep learning to overcome all the challenges stated earlier. The following subsection shows the criteria that need to be satisfied for better performance of distributed deep learning.

Important characteristics for distributed deep learning design

the following are the important characteristics of distributed deep learning design:

1. **Small batch processing**: In distributed deep learning, the network must intake and process data quickly in parallel. To process and provide results more accurately, every node of the cluster should receive small chunks of data of approximately 10 elements at a time.

   For example, say the master node of YARN is coordinating 20 worker nodes for a Big dataset of 200 GB. The master node will split the dataset into 10 GB of 20 small batches of data, allocating one small batch to each worker. The workers will process the data in parallel, and send the results back to the master as soon as it finishes the computing. All these outcomes will be aggregated by the master node, and the average of the results will be finally redistributed to the individual workers.

   Deep learning networks perform well with small batches of nearly 10, rather than working with 100 or 200 large batches of data. Small batches of data empower the networks to learn from different orientations of the data in-depth, which later on recompiles to give a broader knowledge to the model.

   On the other hand, if the batch size is too large, the network tries to learn quickly, which maximizes the errors. Conversly, smaller batch size slows down the speed of learning, and results in the possibility of divergence as the network approaches towards the minimum error rate.

2. **Parameter Averaging**: Parameter averaging is a crucial operation for the training of distributed deep network. In a network, parameters are generally the weight and biases of the node layers. As mentioned in the small batch processing section, once training is completed for several workers, they will pass different sets of parameters back to the master. With every iteration, the parameters are averaged, updated, and sent back to the master for further operations.
   The sequential process of parameter averaging can be outlined as follows:
   - The master configures the initial network and sets the different hyperparameters
   - Based on the configuration of the training master, the Big dataset is split into chunks of several smaller datasets

- For each split of the training dataset, until the error rate approaches towards zero, perform the following:
  - The master distributes the parameter from the master to each individual worker
  - Each worker starts the training of the model with its dedicated chunk of dataset
  - The average of the parameters is calculated and returned back to the master.
- The training completes, and the master will have one copy of the training network

Parameter averaging offers the following two important advantages in case of distributed training:

- It enables parallelism by generating simultaneous results.
- It helps to prevent over-fitting by distributing the given dataset into multiple datasets of smaller sizes. The network then learns the average result, rather than just aggregating the results from different smaller batches.

Figure 2.6 shows a combined diagrammatic overview of the small batch processing and parameter averaging operation:

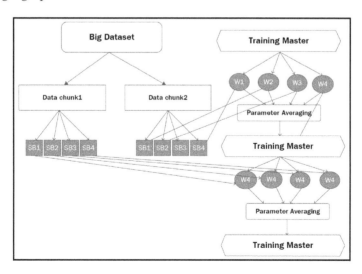

Figure 2.6: Figure shows the high level architecture of a distributed deep learning architecture

Deeplearning4j – an open source distributed framework for deep learning

Deeplearning4j (DL4J) [82] is an open source deep learning framework which is written for JVM, and mainly used for commercial grade. The framework is written entirely in Java, and thus, the name '4j' is included. Because of its use with Java, Deeplearning4j has started to earn popularity with a much wider audience and range of practitioners.

This framework is basically composed of a distributed deep learning library that is integrated with Hadoop and Spark. With the help of Hadoop and Spark, we can very easily distribute the model and Big datasets, and run multiple GPUs and CPUs to perform parallel operations. Deeplearning4j has primarily shown substantial success in performing pattern recognition in images, sound, text, time series data, and so on. Apart from that, it can also be applied for various customer use cases such as facial recognition, fraud detection, business analytics, recommendation engines, image and voice search, and predictive maintenance with the sensor data.

The following *Figure 2.7* shows a generic high-level architectural block diagram of Deeplearning4j:

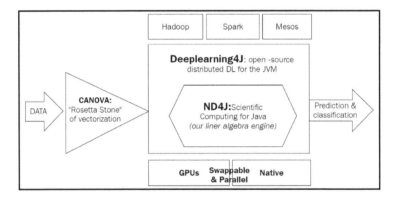

Figure 2.7: High level architectural block diagram of Deeplearning4j [82]

Major features of Deeplearning4j

Deeplearning4j comes with various attractive features, which completely distinguishes it from other existing deep learning tools like Theano, Torch, and so on.

- **Distributed architecture**: Training in Deeplearning4j can be performed in two ways – with distributed, multi-threaded deep-learning, or with traditional, normal single-threaded deep-learning techniques. The training is carried out in clusters of commodity nodes. Therefore, Deeplearning4j is able to process any amount of data quickly. The neural networks are trained in parallel using the iterative reduce method, which works on Hadoop YARN and Spark. It also integrates with Cuda kernels to conduct pure GPU operations, and works with distributed GPUs.

  Deeplearning4j operations can be run on Hadoop YARN or Spark as a job. In Hadoop, Iterative Reduce workers work on every block of HDFS, and synchronously process the data in parallel. As the processing completes, they push the transformed parameters back to their master, where the average of the parameters are taken and the model of each worker's node is updated.

  In Deeplearning4j, the distributed runtimes are interchangeable, where they act like a directory in a huge modular architecture, which can be swapped in or out.

- **Data parallelism**: There are two ways in which the neural networks can be trained in a distributed manner: one is data parallelism, and the other is model parallelism. Deeplearning4j follows data parallelism for training. In data parallelism, we can split the large dataset into chunks of smaller datasets, and distribute those to parallel models running on different servers to train in parallel.

- **Scientific computing capability for the JVM**: For scientific computing in Java and Scala, Deeplearning4j includes an N-dimensional array class using **N-Dimensional Arrays for Java** (**ND4J**). The functionality of ND4J is much faster than what Numpy provides to Python, and its mostly written in C++. It's effectively based on a library for matrix manipulation and linear algebra in a production environment. Most of the routines of ND4J are designed to run fast with minimum RAM requirements.

- **Vectorization tool for machine learning**: For vectorization of various file formats and data types, Canova has been merged with Deeplearning4j. Canova performs vectorization using an input/output system similar to how Hadoop uses Map-Reduce. Canova is primarily designed to vectorize text, CSVs, images, sounds, videos, and so on from the **command line interface** (**CLI**).

Summary of functionalities of Deeplearning4j

The following are summary of functionalities of Deeplearning4j:

- Deeplearning4j can be claimed as the most complete, production-ready, open source deep learning library ever built
- Compared to Theano-based tools, it has many more features specially designed for deep networks
- Deeplearning4j is very easy to use; even non-specialists can apply its conventions to solve computationally intensive problems
- The tools provide a wide range of applicability, hence, the networks work equally well with image, sound, text, and time-series
- It is completely distributed and can run multiple GPUs in parallel, unlike Theano [84], which is not distributed, and Torch7 [85], which has not automated its distribution like DL4J

Setting up Deeplearning4j on Hadoop YARN

Deeplearning4j primarily works on networks having multiple layers. To get started working with Deeplearning4j, one needs to get accustomed with the prerequisites, and how to install all the dependent software. Most of the documentation can be easily found on the official website of Deeplearning4j at `https://deeplearning4j.org/` [88].

In this section of the chapter, we will help you to get familiar with the code of Deeplearning4j. Initially, we will show the implementation of a simple operation of a multilayer neural network with Deeplearning4j. The later part of the section will discuss distributed deep learning with Deeplearning4j library. Deeplearning4j trains distributed deep neural network on multiple distributed GPUs using Apache Spark. The later part of this section will also introduce the setup of Apache Spark for Deeplearning4j.

Getting familiar with Deeplearning4j

This part will mainly introduce the 'Hello World' programs of deep learning with deeplearning4j. We will explain the basic functions of the library with the help of two simple deep learning problems.

In Deeplearning4j, `MultiLayerConfiguration`, a class of the library can be considered as the base of the building block, which is responsible for organizing the layers and the corresponding hyperparameters of a neural network. This class can be considered as the core building block of Deeplearning4j for neural networks. Throughout the book, we will use this class to configure different multilayer neural networks.

 Hyperparameters are the main backbone to determine the learning process of a neural network. They mostly include how to initialize the weights of the models, how many times they should be updated, the learning rate of the model, which optimization algorithms to use, and so on.

In the first example, we will show how to classify data patterns for the multilayer perceptron classifier with the help of Deeplearning4j.

The following is the sample training dataset that will be used in this program:

```
0, -0.500568579838,  0.687106471955
1,  0.190067977988, -0.341116711905
0,  0.995019651532,  0.663292952846
0, -1.03053733564,   0.342392729177
1,  0.0376749555484,-0.836548188848
0, -0.113745482508,  0.740204108847
1,  0.56769119889,  -0.375810486522
```

Initially, we need to initialize the various hyperparameters of the networks. The following piece of code will set the ND4J environment for the program:

```
Nd4j.ENFORCE_NUMERICAL_STABILITY = true;
int batchSize = 50;
int seed = 123;
double learningRate = 0.005;
```

Number of epochs is set to `30`:

```
int nEpochs = 30;
int numInputs = 2;
int numOutputs = 2;
int numHiddenNodes = 20;
```

The following piece of code will load the training data to the network:

```
RecordReader rr = new CSVRecordReader();
rr.initialize(new FileSplit(new File("saturn_data_train.csv")));
DataSetIterator trainIter = new RecordReaderDataSetIterator
                            (rr,batchSize,0,2);
```

As the training data is loaded next we load the test data into the model with the following code:

```
RecordReader rrTest = new CSVRecordReader();
rrTest.initialize(new FileSplit(new File("saturn_data_eval.csv")));
DataSetIterator trainIter = new RecordReaderDataSetIterator
                                   (rrTest,batchSize,0,2);
```

Organization of all the layers of the network model as well as setting up the hyperparameters can be done with the following piece of code:

```
MultiLayerConfiguration conf = new NeuralNetConfiguration.Builder()
.seed(seed)
.iterations(1)
.optimizationAlgo(OptimizationAlgorithm.STOCHASTIC_GRADIENT_DESCENT)
.learningRate(learningRate)
.updater(Updater.NESTEROVS).momentum(0.9)
.list()
.layer(0, new DenseLayer.Builder().nIn(numInputs).nOut(numHiddenNodes)
    .weightInit(WeightInit.XAVIER)
    .activation("relu")
    .build())
.layer(1, new OutputLayer.Builder(LossFunction.NEGATIVELOGLIKELIHOOD)
    .weightInit(WeightInit.XAVIER)
    .activation("softmax")
    .nIn(numHiddenNodes).nOut(numOutputs).build())
.pretrain(false)
.backprop(true)
.build();
```

Now, we have loaded the training and test dataset, the initialization of the model can be done by calling the `init()` method. This will also start the training of the model from the given inputs:

```
MultiLayerNetwork model = new MultiLayerNetwork(conf);
model.init();
```

To check the output after a certain internal, let's print the scores every 5 parameter updates:

```
model.setListeners(new ScoreIterationListener(5));
for ( int n = 0; n < nEpochs; n++)
{
```

Finally, the network is trained by calling the `.fit()` method:

```
    model.fit( trainIter );
}
System.out.println("Evaluating the model....");
Evaluation eval = new Evaluation(numOutputs);
while(testIter.hasNext())
  {
    DataSet t = testIter.next();
    INDArray features = t.getFeatureMatrix();
    INDArray lables = t.getLabels();
    INDArray predicted = model.output(features,false);
    eval.eval(lables, predicted);
  }
System.out.println(eval.stats());
```

So the training of the model is done. In the next part, the data points will be plotted and the corresponding accuracy of the data will be calculated as shown in the following code:

```
double xMin = -15;
double xMax = 15;
double yMin = -15;
double yMax = 15;

int nPointsPerAxis = 100;
double[][] evalPoints = new double[nPointsPerAxis*nPointsPerAxis][2];
int count = 0;
for( int i=0; i<nPointsPerAxis; i++ )
{
 for( int j=0; j<nPointsPerAxis; j++ )
 {
    double x = i * (xMax-xMin)/(nPointsPerAxis-1) + xMin;
    double y = j * (yMax-yMin)/(nPointsPerAxis-1) + yMin;

    evalPoints[count][0] = x;
    evalPoints[count][1] = y;

    count++;
 }
}

INDArray allXYPoints = Nd4j.create(evalPoints);

INDArray predictionsAtXYPoints = model.output(allXYPoints);
```

The following code will store all the training data in an array before plotting those in the graph:

```
rr.initialize(new FileSplit(new File("saturn_data_train.csv")));
rr.reset();
int nTrainPoints = 500;
trainIter = new RecordReaderDataSetIterator(rr,nTrainPoints,0,2);
DataSet ds = trainIter.next();
PlotUtil.plotTrainingData(ds.getFeatures(), ds.getLabels(),allXYPoints,
predictionsAtXYPoints, nPointsPerAxis);
```

Running the test data through the network and generating the prediction can be done with the following code:

```
rrTest.initialize(new FileSplit(new File("saturn_data_eval.csv")));
rrTest.reset();
int nTestPoints = 100;
testIter = new RecordReaderDataSetIterator(rrTest,nTestPoints,0,2);
ds = testIter.next();
INDArray testPredicted = model.output(ds.getFeatures());
PlotUtil.plotTestData(ds.getFeatures(), ds.getLabels(), testPredicted,
allXYPoints, predictionsAtXYPoints, nPointsPerAxis);
```

When the preceding code is executed, it will run for approximately 5-10 seconds, depending upon your system configuration. During that time, you can check the console, which will display the updated score of training for your model.

A piece of evaluation is displayed as follows:

```
o.d.o.l.ScoreIterationListener - Score at iteration 0 is
                                 0.6313823699951172
o.d.o.l.ScoreIterationListener - Score at iteration 5 is
                                 0.6154170989990234
o.d.o.l.ScoreIterationListener - Score at iteration 10 is
                                 0.4763660430908203
o.d.o.l.ScoreIterationListener - Score at iteration 15 is
                                 0.52469970703125
o.d.o.l.ScoreIterationListener - Score at iteration 20 is
                                 0.4296367645263672
o.d.o.l.ScoreIterationListener - Score at iteration 25 is
                                 0.4755714416503906
o.d.o.l.ScoreIterationListener - Score at iteration 30 is
                                 0.3985047912597656
o.d.o.l.ScoreIterationListener - Score at iteration 35 is
                                 0.4304619598388672
o.d.o.l.ScoreIterationListener - Score at iteration 40 is
                                 0.3672477722167969
o.d.o.l.ScoreIterationListener - Score at iteration 45 is
```

```
                                  0.39150180816650393
o.d.o.l.ScoreIterationListener - Score at iteration 50 is
                                  0.3353725051879883
o.d.o.l.ScoreIterationListener - Score at iteration 55 is
                                  0.3596681213378906
```

Finally, the program will output the different statistics of the training for the model using Deeplearning4j as follows:

```
Evaluating the model....
Examples labeled as 0 classified by model as 0: 48 times
Examples labeled as 1 classified by model as 1: 52 times
```

In the background, we can visualize the plotting of the data, which will give an impression of what the planet Saturn looks like. In the next part, we will show how to integrate Hadoop YARN and Spark with Deeplearning4j. The following *Figure 2.8* shows the output of the program in graphical representation:

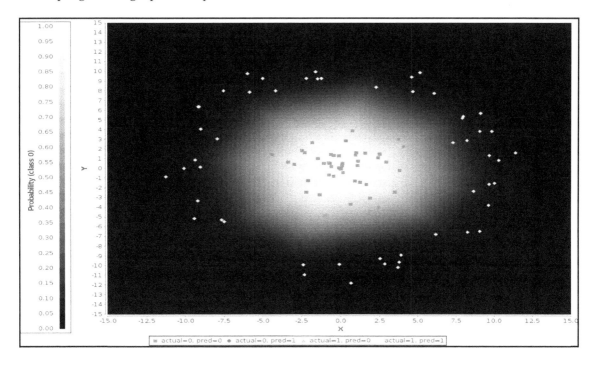

Figure 2.8: The scattered data points are plotted when the preceding program is executed. The data points give an impression of the planet Saturn

Integration of Hadoop YARN and Spark for distributed deep learning

To use Deeplearning4j on Hadoop, we need to include the `deeplearning-hadoop` dependency as shown in the following code:

```
<!--
https://mvnrepository.com/artifact/org.Deeplearning4j/Deeplearning4j-hadoop
-->
<dependency>
    <groupId>org.Deeplearning4j</groupId>
    <artifactId>Deeplearning4j-hadoop</artifactId>
    <version>0.0.3.2.7</version>
</dependency>
```

Similarly, for Spark, we have to include the `deeplearning-spark` dependency as shown in the following code:

```
<!--
https://mvnrepository.com/artifact/org.Deeplearning4j/dl4j-spark-nlp_2.11 -
-->
<dependency>
    <groupId>org.Deeplearning4j</groupId>
    <artifactId>dl4j-spark-nlp_2.11</artifactId>
    <version>0.5.0</version>
</dependency>
```

Explaining the detailed functionalities of Apache Spark is beyond the scope of this book. Interested readers can catch up on the same at `http://spark.apache.org/`.

Rules to configure memory allocation for Spark on Hadoop YARN

As already stated in the previous section, Apache Hadoop YARN is a cluster resource manager. When Deeplearning4j submits a training job to a YARN cluster via Spark, it is the responsibility of YARN to manage the allocation of resources such as CPU cores, amount of memory consumed by each executor, and so on. However, to extract the best performance from Deeplearning4j on YARN, some careful memory configuration is desired. This is done as follows:

- The executer JVM memory amount needs to be specified using `spark.executor.memory`.

- The YARN container memory overhead needs to be specified using `spark.yarn.executor.memoryOverhead`.
- The sum of `spark.executor.memory` and `spark.yarn.executor.memoryOverhead` must always be less than the amount of memory allocated to a container by the YARN.
- ND4j and JavaCPP should know the allotment of the off-heap memory; this can be done using the `org.bytedeco.javacpp.maxbytes` system property.
- `org.bytedeco.javacpp.maxbytes` must be less than `spark.yarn.executor.memoryOverhead`.

The current version of Deeplearning4j uses parameter averaging to perform distributed training of the neural network. The following operation is performed exactly the way it is described in the parameter averaging part of the earlier section:

```
SparkDl4jMultiLayer sparkNet = new SparkDl4jMultiLayer(sc,conf,
                          new ParameterAveragingTrainingMaster
                          .Builder(numExecutors(),dataSetObjSize
                          .batchSizePerWorker(batchSizePerExecutor)
                          .averagingFrequency(1)
                          .repartionData(Repartition.Always)
                          .build());
sparkNet.setCollectTrainingStats(true);
```

To list all the files from HDFS so as to run the code on different nodes, run the following code:

```
Configuration config = new Configuration();
FileSystem hdfs = FileSystem.get(tempDir.toUri(), config);
RemoteIterator<LocatedFileStatus> fileIter = hdfs.listFiles
   (new org.apache.hadoop.fs.Path(tempDir.toString()),false);

List<String> paths = new ArrayList<>();
while(fileIter.hasNext())
   {
    String path = fileIter.next().getPath().toString();
    paths.add(path);
   }
```

A complete code for how to set up Spark with YARN and HDFS will be provided along with the code bundle. For simplicity, only part of the code is shown here for the purpose of understanding.

Now, we will show an example to demonstrate how to use Spark and load the data into memory with Deeplearning4j. We will use a basic DataVec example to show some pre-processing operation on some CSV data.

The sample dataset will look as like the following:

```
2016-01-01 17:00:00.000,830a7u3,u323fy8902,1,USA,100.00,Legit
2016-01-01 18:03:01.256,830a7u3,9732498oeu,3,FR,73.20,Legit
2016-01-03 02:53:32.231,78ueoau32,w234e989,1,USA,1621.00,Fraud
2016-01-03 09:30:16.832,t842uocd,9732498oeu,4,USA,43.19,Legit
2016-01-04 23:01:52.920,t842uocd,cza8873bm,10,MX,159.65,Legit
2016-01-05 02:28:10.648,t842uocd,fgcq9803,6,CAN,26.33,Fraud
2016-01-05 10:15:36.483,rgc707ke3,tn342v7,2,USA,-0.90,Legit
```

The problem statement of the program is as follows:

- Remove some unnecessary columns
- Filter out data, and keep only examples with values USA and MX for the MerchantCountryCode column
- Replace the invalid entries in the TransactionAmountUSD column
- Parse the data string, and collect the hour of day from it to create a new HourOfDay column

```
Schema inputDataSchema = new Schema.Builder()
    .addColumnString("DateTimeString")
    .addColumnsString("CustomerID", "MerchantID")
    .addColumnInteger("NumItemsInTransaction")
    .addColumnCategorical("MerchantCountryCode",
     Arrays.asList("USA","CAN","FR","MX"))
    .addColumnDouble("TransactionAmountUSD",0.0,null,false,false)
    .addColumnCategorical("FraudLabel",Arrays.asList("Fraud","Legit"))
    .build();
System.out.println("\n\nOther information obtainable from schema:");
System.out.println("Number of columns: " +
                inputDataSchema.numColumns());
System.out.println("Column names: " +
                inputDataSchema.getColumnNames());
System.out.println("Column types: " +
                inputDataSchema.getColumnTypes());
```

The following part will define the operations that we want to perform on the dataset:

```
TransformProcess tp = new TransformProcess.Builder(inputDataSchema)
.removeColumns("CustomerID","MerchantID")
.filter(new ConditionFilter(
 new CategoricalColumnCondition("MerchantCountryCode",
```

```
ConditionOp.NotInSet, new HashSet<>(Arrays.asList("USA","MX")))))
```

In unstructured data, the datasets are generally noisy, and so we need to take care of some of the invalid data. In case of negative dollar value, the program will replace those to 0.0. We will keep the positive dollar amounts intact.

```
.conditionalReplaceValueTransform(
  "TransactionAmountUSD",
  new DoubleWritable(0.0),
  new DoubleColumnCondition("TransactionAmountUSD",ConditionOp.LessThan
  , 0.0))
```

Now, to format the DateTime format as per the problem statement, the following piece of code is used:

```
.stringToTimeTransform("DateTimeString","YYYY-MM-DD HH:mm:ss.SSS",
 DateTimeZone.UTC)
.renameColumn("DateTimeString", "DateTime")
.transform(new DeriveColumnsFromTimeTransform.Builder("DateTime")
  .addIntegerDerivedColumn("HourOfDay", DateTimeFieldType.hourOfDay())
  .build())
.removeColumns("DateTime")
.build();
```

A different schema is created after execution of the all these operations as follows:

```
Schema outputSchema = tp.getFinalSchema();

System.out.println("\nSchema after transforming data:");
System.out.println(outputSchema);
```

The following piece of code will set Spark to perform all the operations:

```
SparkConf conf = new SparkConf();
conf.setMaster("local[*]");
conf.setAppName("DataVec Example");

JavaSparkContext sc = new JavaSparkContext(conf);

String directory = new  ClassPathResource("exampledata.csv").getFile()
.getParent();
```

To take the data directly from HDFS, one has to pass `hdfs://{the filepath name}`:

```
JavaRDD<String> stringData = sc.textFile(directory);
```

The input data are parsed using `CSVRecordReader()` method as follows:

```
RecordReader rr = new CSVRecordReader();
JavaRDD<List<Writable>> parsedInputData = stringData.map(new
StringToWritablesFunction(rr));
```

The pre-defined transformation of Spark is performed as follows:

```
SparkTransformExecutor exec = new SparkTransformExecutor();
JavaRDD<List<Writable>> processedData = exec.execute(parsedInputData,
tp);
JavaRDD<String> processedAsString = processedData.map(new
WritablesToStringFunction(","));
```

As mentioned, to save the data back to HDFS, just putting the file path after `hdfs://` will do:

```
processedAsString.saveAsTextFile("hdfs://your/hdfs/save/path/here")

List<String> processedCollected = processedAsString.collect();
List<String> inputDataCollected = stringData.collect();


System.out.println("\n ---- Original Data ----");
for(String s : inputDataCollected) System.out.println(s);

System.out.println("\n ---- Processed Data ----");
for(String s : processedCollected) System.out.println(s);
```

When the program is executed with Spark using Deeplearning4j, we will get the following output:

```
14:20:12 INFO MemoryStore: Block broadcast_0 stored as values in memory
(estimated size 104.0 KB, free 1390.9 MB)
16/08/27 14:20:12 INFO MemoryStore: ensureFreeSpace(10065) called with
curMem=106480, maxMem=1458611159
16/08/27 14:20:12 INFO MemoryStore: Block broadcast_0_piece0 stored as
bytes in memory (estimated size 9.8 KB, free 1390.9 MB)
16/08/27 14:20:12 INFO BlockManagerInfo: Added broadcast_0_piece0 in memory
on localhost:46336 (size: 9.8 KB, free: 1391.0 MB)
16/08/27 14:20:12 INFO SparkContext: Created broadcast 0 from textFile at
BasicDataVecExample.java:144
16/08/27 14:20:13 INFO SparkTransformExecutor: Starting execution of stage
1 of 7
```

```
16/08/27 14:20:13 INFO SparkTransformExecutor: Starting execution of stage
2 of 7
16/08/27 14:20:13 INFO SparkTransformExecutor: Starting execution of stage
3 of 7
16/08/27 14:20:13 INFO SparkTransformExecutor: Starting execution of stage
4 of 7
16/08/27 14:20:13 INFO SparkTransformExecutor: Starting execution of stage
5 of 7
```

The following is the output:

```
---- Processed Data ----
17,1,USA,100.00,Legit
2,1,USA,1621.00,Fraud
9,4,USA,43.19,Legit
23,10,MX,159.65,Legit
10,2,USA,0.0,Legit
```

Similar to this example, lots of other datasets can be processed in a customized way in Spark. From the next chapter, we will show the Deeplearning4j codes for specific deep neural networks. The implementation of Apache Spark and Hadoop YARN is a generic procedure, and will not change according to neural network. Readers can use that code to deploy the deep network code in cluster or locally, based on their requirements.

Summary

In contrast to the traditional machine learning algorithms, deep learning models have the capability to address the challenges imposed by a massive amount of input data. Deep learning networks are designed to automatically extract complex representation of data from the unstructured data. This property makes deep learning a precious tool to learn the hidden information from the big data. However, due to the velocity at which the volume and varieties of data are increasing day by day, deep learning networks need to be stored and processed in a distributed manner. Hadoop, being the most widely used big data framework for such requirements, is extremely convenient in this situation. We explained the primary components of Hadoop that are essential for distributed deep learning architecture. The crucial characteristics of distributed deep learning networks were also explained in depth. Deeplearning4j, an open source distributed deep learning framework, integrates with Hadoop to achieve the mentioned indispensable requirement.

Deeplearning4j is entirely written in Java, can process data faster in a distributed manner with iterative Map-Reduce, and can address many problems imposed by the large-scale data. We have provided two sample examples to let you know about basic Deeplearning4j codes and syntax. We have also provided some code snippets for Spark configuration with integration with Hadoop YARN and Hadoop Distributed File System.

The next chapter of this book will introduce convolutional neural network, a popular deep learning network. The chapter will discuss the method convolution and how it can be used to build an advanced neural network mainly for image processing and image recognition. The chapter will then provide information on how a convolutional neural network can be implemented using Deeplearning4j.

3

Convolutional Neural Network

"The question of whether a computer can think is no more interesting than the question of whether a submarine can swim."

– Edsger W. Dijkstra

Convolutional neural network (CNN)–doesn't it give an uncanny feeling about the combination of mathematics and biology with some negligible amount of computer science added? However, these type of networks have been some of the most dominant and powerful architectures in the field of computer vision. CNN started to gain its popularity after 2012, when there were huge improvements in the precision of classification, credit to some pioneer in the field of deep learning. Ever since then, a bunch of high-tech companies have been using deep CNN for various services. Amazon uses CNN for their product recommendations, Google uses it for their photo search, and Facebook primarily uses it for its automatic tagging algorithms.

CNN [89] is a type of feed-forward neural network comprised of neurons, which have learnable weights and biases. These types of networks are basically used to process data, having the grid-like topology form. CNNs, as the name suggests, are a type of neural network where, unlike the general matrix multiplication, a special type of linear mathematical operation, convolution, is used in at least one of the subsequent layers. The architecture of CNN is designed to take the benefit of input with multidimensional structure. These include the 2D structure of an input image, speech signal, or even one-dimensional time series data. With all these advantages, CNN has been really successful with many practical applications. CNN is thus tremendously successful, specifically in fields such as natural language processing, recommender systems, image recognition, and video recognition.

A bias unit is an *extra* neuron that has a value of 1 and is added to each pre-output layer. These units are not connected to the previous layer and so do not represent any *activity* in a real sense.

In this chapter, we will discuss the building block of CNN in-depth. We will initially discuss what convolution is and the need of convolution operations in the neural network. Under that topic, we will also address pooling operation, which is the most important component of CNN. The next topic of this chapter will point out the major challenges of CNN while dealing with large-scale data. The last part of this chapter will help the reader to learn how to design CNN using Deeplearning4j.

The main topics of the chapter are listed as follows:

- Understanding convolution
- Background of a CNN
- Basic layers of CNN
- Distributed deep CNN
- CNN with Deeplearning4j

Understanding convolution

To understand the concept of convolution, let us take an example to determine the position of a lost mobile phone with the help of a laser sensor. Let's say the current location of the mobile phone at time t can be given by the laser as $f(t)$. The laser gives different readings of the location for all the values of t. The laser sensors are generally noisy in nature, which is undesirable for this scenario. Therefore, to derive a less noisy measurement of the location of the phone, we need to calculate the average various measurements. Ideally, the more the measurements, the greater the accuracy of the location. Hence, we should undergo a weighted average, which provides more weight to the measurements.

A weighted function can be given by the function $w(b)$, where b denotes the age of the measurement. To derive a new function that will provide a better estimate of the location of the mobile phone, we need to take the average of the weight at every moment.

The new function can be given as follows:

$$g(t) = \int f(b)w(t-b)db$$

The preceding operation is termed as convolution. The conventional method of representing convolution is denoted by an asterisk or star, '*':

$$g\ (t)\ =\ (f^{*}w)\ (t)$$

Formally, convolution can be defined as an integral of the product of two functions, where one of the functions is reversed and shifted. Besides, taking the weighted averages, it may also be used for other purposes.

In terms of convolutional network terminology, the function f in our example is referred to as the input and the function w, the second parameter is called the kernel of the operation. The kernel is composed of a number of filters, which will be used on the input to get the output, referred to as *feature maps*. In a more convenient way, the kernel can be seen as a membrane, which will allow only the desirable features of the input to pass through it. *Figure 3.1* shows a pictorial view of the operation:

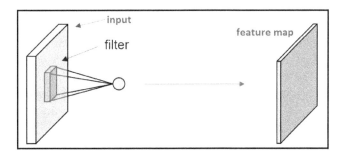

Figure 3.1: The figure shows a simple representation of a convolutional network where the input has to pass through the kernel to provide the feature map.

In a practical scenario, as our example shows, the laser sensor cannot really provide the measurements at every given instant of time. Ideally, when a computer works on data, it only works at some regular intervals; hence, the time will be discrete. So, the sensor will generally provide the results at some defined interval of time. If we assume that the instrument provides output once/second, then the parameter t will only take integer values. With these assumptions, the functions f and w will only be defined for integer values of t. The modified equation for discrete convolution can now be written as follows:

$$g(t) = (f * w)(t) = \sum_{b=-\infty}^{\infty} f(b)w(t-b)$$

In case of machine learning or deep learning applications, the inputs are generally a multidimensional array of data, and the kernel uses multidimensional arrays of different parameters taken by the algorithm. The basic assumption is that the values of the functions are non-zero only for a finite set of points for which we store the values, and zero elsewhere. So, the infinite summation can be represented as the summation for a range of a finite number of array elements. For example, for a 2D image I as an input and a corresponding 2D kernel K, the convolution function can be written as follows:

$$S(p,q) = (I * K)(p,q) = \sum_a \sum_b I(a,b)K(p-a)(q-b)$$

So, with this, you have already got some background of convolution. In the next section of this chapter, we will discuss the application of convolution in a neural network and the building blocks of CNN.

Background of a CNN

CNN, a particular form of deep learning models, is not a new concept, and they have been widely adopted by the vision community for a long time. The model worked well in recognizing the hand-written digit by LeCun et al in 1998 [90]. But unfortunately, due to the inability of CNNs to work with higher resolution images, its popularity has diminished with the course of time. The reason was mostly due to hardware and memory constraints, and also the lack of availability of large-scale training datasets. As the computational power increases with time, mostly due to the wide availability of CPUs and GPUs and with the generation of big data, various large-scale datasets, such as the MIT Places dataset (see Zhou et al., 2014), ImageNet [91] and so on. it became possible to train larger and complex models. This is initially shown by Krizhevsky et al [4] in their paper, *Imagenet classification using deep convolutional neural networks*. In that paper, they brought down the error rate with half-beating traditional approaches. Over the next few years, their paper became one of the most substantial papers in the field of computer vision. This popular network trained by Alex Krizhevsky, called AlexNet, could well have been the starting point of using deep networks in the field of computer vision.

Architecture overview

We assume that the readers are already familiar with the traditional neural network. In this section, we will look at the general building blocks of CNN.

The traditional neural network receives a single vector as input, and reaches the intermediate states through a series of latent (hidden) layers. Each hidden layer is composed of several neurons, where each neuron is fully connected to every other neuron of the previous layer. The last layer, called the 'output layer', is fully-connected, and it is responsible for the class scores. A regular neural network composed of three layers is shown in *Figure 3.2*:

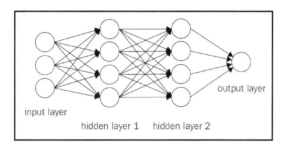

Figure 3.2: The figure shows the block diagram of a three-layer regular neural network. The neurons of every layer are fully-connected to every other layer of the previous layer.

Regular neural networks face tremendous challenges while dealing with large-scale images. For example, in the CIFAR-10 RGB database, the dimension of the images are *32x32x3*, hence, a single fully-connected neuron in a first hidden layer of the traditional neural network will have *32*32*3= 3072* number of weights. The number of weights, although seems to be reasonable at the outset, would really be a cumbersome task to manage with the increasing number of dimensions. For another RGB image, if the dimension becomes (*300x300x3*), the total number of weights of the neurons will result in *300*300*3 = 270000* weights. Also, as the number of layers will increase, this number will also increase drastically, and would quickly lead to overfitting. Moreover, visualization of an image completely neglects the complex 2D spatial structure of the image. Therefore, the fully-connected concept of the neural network, right from the initial phase, does not seem to work with the larger dimensional datasets. So, we need to build a model that will overcome both of these limitations:

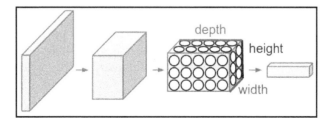

Figure 3.3: The arrangement of CNN in 3D (width, height, and depth) is represented in the figure. Every layer converts the 3D input volume to the corresponding 3D output volume of neuron activations. The red input layer keeps the image, hence, its width and height would be the dimensions of the image, where the depth would be three (Red, Green, and Blue). Image sourced from Wikipedia.

One way to solve this problem is to use convolution in place of matrix multiplication. Learning from a set of convolutional filters (kernel) is much easier than learning from the whole matrix (*300x300x3*). Unlike the traditional neural network, the layers of a CNN have their neurons arranged in three dimensions: width, height, and depth. *Figure 3.3* shows the representation for this. For example, in the previous example of CIFAR-10, the image has a dimension of *32x32x3*, which is width, depth, and height respectively. In a CNN, instead of the neurons in a fully-connected nature, the neurons in a layer will only be connected to a subset of neurons in the previous layer. Details of this will be explained in the subsequent portion of this section. Moreover, the final output layer CIFAR-10 image will have the dimension *1x1x10*, because the CNN will diminish the full image into a single vector of class score, placed along with the depth dimension.

Basic layers of CNN

A CNN is composed of a sequence of layers, where every layer of the network goes through a differentiable function to transform itself from one volume of activation to another. Four main types of layers are used to build a CNN: Convolutional layer, Rectified Linear Units layer, Pooling layer, and Fully-connected layer. All these layers are stacked together to form a full CNN.

A regular CNN could have the following architecture:

[INPUT – CONV – RELU – POOL – FC]

However, in a deep CNN, there are generally more layers interspersed between these five basic layers.

A classic deep neural network will have the following structure:

Input -> Conv->ReLU->Conv->ReLu->Pooling->ReLU->Conv->ReLu->Pooling->Fully Connected

AlexNet, as mentioned in the earlier section, can be taken as a perfect example for this kind of structure. The architecture of AlexNet is shown in *Figure 3.4*. After every layer, an implicit ReLU non-linearity has been added. We will explain this in detail in the next section.

One might wonder, why do we need multiple layers in a CNN? The next section of this chapter shall explain this as well:

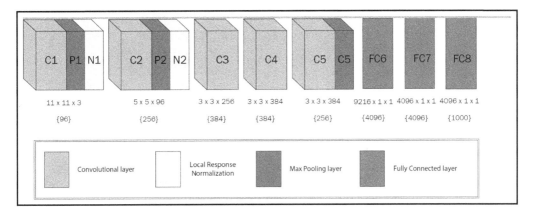

Figure 3.4: An illustration of the depth and weight of the AlexNet is shown in the figure. The number inside the curly braces denotes the number of filters with dimensions written above.

Importance of depth in a CNN

In the paper [96], the author has put forward a few statistics, to show how deep networks help in gaining more accuracy of the output. As noted, the Architecture of Krizhevsky et al. model uses eight layers, which are trained on ImageNet. When the fully connected top layer (7th layer) is removed, it drops approximately 16 million parameters with a performance drop of 1.1%. Furthermore, when the top two layers (6th and 7th) are removed, nearly 50 million parameters get reduced along with a 5.7% drop in performance. Similarly, when the upper feature extractor layers (3rd and 4th) are removed, it results in a drop of around 1 million parameters with a performance drop of 3.0%. To get a better insight of the scenario, when the upper feature extractor layers and the fully connected (3rd, 4th, 6th, and 7th) layers are removed, the model was left with only four layers. In that case, a 33.5% drop in performance is experienced.

Therefore, it can be easily concluded that we need deep convolutional network to increase the performance of the model. However, as already stated, a deep network is extremely difficult to manage in a centralized system due to limitations of memory and performance management. So, a distributed way of implementing deep CNN is required. In the subsequent sections of this chapter, we will explain how to implement this with the help of Deeplearning4j, and integrating the processing with Hadoop's YARN.

Convolutional layer

As illustrated in the architecture overview, the main purpose of convolution is to allow the model to work with a limited number of inputs at a particular time. Moreover, convolution supports three most important features, which substantially help in improving the performance of a deep learning model. The features are listed as follows:

- Sparse connectivity
- Parameter sharing
- Equivariant representations

We will now describe each of these features in turn.

Sparse connectivity

As already explained, the traditional network layers use matrix multiplication by a matrix of parameters with a different parameter describing the interaction between each output unit and input unit. On the other hand, CNNs use sparse connectivity, sometimes referred to as sparse interactions or sparse weights, for this purpose. This idea is attained by keeping the size of the kernel smaller than the input, which helps in reducing the time complexity of the algorithm. For example, for a large image dataset, the image could have thousands or millions of pixels; however, we can identify the small, significant features of the image, such as edges and contours from the kernels, which only have hundreds or tens of the whole pixels. Therefore, we need to keep only a small number of parameters, which, in turn, helps in the reduction of memory requirements of the models and datasets. The idea also alleviates the number of operations, which could enhance the overall computing power. This, in turn, decreases the running time complexity of the computation in a huge manner, which eventually ameliorates its efficiency. *Figure 3.5* diagrammatically shows, how with the sparse connectivity approach, we can reduce the number of receptive fields of each neuron.

Each neuron in a Convolutional layer renders the response of the filters applied in the previous layer. The main purpose of these neurons is to pass the responses through some non-linearity. The total area of the previous layers, where that filter was applied, is termed as the receptive field of that neuron. So, the receptive field is always equivalent to the size of the filter.

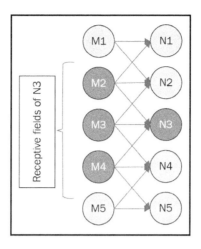

Figure 3.5: The figure shows how the input units of M affect the output unit N3 with sparse connectivity.Unlike matrix multiplication, the number of receptive fields in the sparse connectivity approach reduce from five to three (M2, M3, and M4). The arrows indicate the parameter sharing approach too. The connections from one neuron are shared with two neurons in the model

Therefore, with the sparse connectivity approach, the receptive fields for each layer are smaller than the receptive fields using the matrix multiplication approach. However, it is to be noted that for deep CNNs, the receptive field of the units is virtually larger than the receptive fields of the corresponding shallow networks. The reason is that all the units in the deep networks are indirectly connected to almost all the neurons of the network. *Figure 3.6* shows a visual representation of such a scenario:

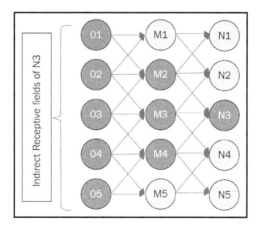

Figure 3.6: Representation of sparse connectivity for deep layers of convolution neural networks. Unlike Figure 3.5, where unit N3 had three receptive fields, here the number of receptive fields of N3 has increased to five.

Improved time complexity

Similar to the example given in the previous section, if there are p inputs and q outputs in a layer, then the matrix multiplication will require $(p*q)$ number of parameters. The running time complexity of the algorithm will become $O\ (p*q)$. With the sparsely connected approach, if we limit the number of upper limit connections associated with each output to n, then it will need only $n*q$ parameters, and the runtime complexity will reduce to $O\ (n*q)$. For many real-life applications, the sparse connectivity approach provides good performance for the deep learning tasks while keeping the size of $n \ll p$.

Parameter sharing

Parameter sharing can be defined as the process by which the same parameter for a function can be used for multiple functions in the model. In regular neural networks, each element of the weight matrix is applied exactly once, when calculating the output of a layer. The weight is multiplied by one element of the input, but never revisited. Parameter sharing can also be referred to as tied weights, as the value of the weight used to one input is tied to the value weight used for others. *Figure 3.5* can also be viewed as an example for parameter sharing. For example, a particular parameter from **M2** is used with both **N1** and **N3**.

The main purpose of the operation is to control the number of free parameters in the Convolutional layer. In a CNN, each element of the kernel is used at almost every position of the input. One logical assumption for this is that if one of the features is desirable at some spatial position, then it should also be necessary to calculate the other positions.

Since all the elements of a single depth slice share the same type of parametrization, the forward pass in each depth slice of the Convolutional layer can be measured as a convolutional of input volume with the weights of the neurons. The outcome of this convolution is an activation map. These collections of activation maps are stacked together with the association of depth dimension to result the output volume. Although the parameter sharing approach bestows the translation invariance of the CNN architecture, it does not enhance the runtime of forward propagation.

Improved space complexity

In parameter sharing, the runtime of the model still remains $O\ (n*q)$. However, it helps to reduce the overall space complexity in a significant way, as the storage requirement of the model reduces to n number of parameters. Since p and q are generally of similar sizes, the value of n becomes almost negligible as compared to $p*q$.

Convolution is considerably more productive than the traditional dense matrix multiplication approach, both in terms of time complexity as well as space complexity.

Equivariant representations

In the convolution layer, due to parameter sharing, the layers possess a property termed as equivariance to translation. An equivariant function is defined as a function whose output changes in the same way the input does.

Mathematically, if X and Y both belong to a same group G, then a function *f: X â→ Y* is said to be equivariant if *f (g.x) = g.f(x) for all gâ→ G* and all *x* in X.

In case of convolution, if we take *g* to be any function, which shifts the input in equal magnitude, then the convolution function is equivariant to *g*. For example, let *I* be a function that gives the image color for any even coordinate. Let *h* be another function, which maps one image function to another image function, given by the following equation:

$$I' = h(I)$$

I' is an image function that moves every pixel of *I* five units to the right. Therefore, we have the following:

$$I'(i,j) = (i - 5, j)$$

Now, if we apply this translation to *I*, followed by the convolution, the result would be exactly the same when we apply convolution to *I'*, followed by the transformation function *h* to the output.

In case of images, a convolution operation generates a two-dimensional map of all the definite features present in the input. So, similar to the earlier example, if we shift the object in the output by some fixed scale, the output representation will also move in the same scale. This concept is useful for some cases; for example, consider a group photo of cricket players of two different teams. We can find some common feature of the jersey in the image to detect some players. Now, the similar feature will obviously be present in others' t-shirts as well. So, it is quite practical to share the parameter across the entire image.

Convolution also helps to process some special kinds of data, which are difficult, or rather not even possible, with the traditional fixed-shape matrix multiplication approach.

Choosing the hyperparameters for Convolutional layers

So far we have explained how each neuron in the convolution layers is connected to the input volume. In this section, we will discuss the ways of controlling the size of the output volume. In other words, controlling the number of neurons in the output volume, and how they are arranged.

Basically, there are three hyperparameters, which control the size of the output volume of the Convolutional layers. They are: the depth, stride, and zero-padding.

How do we know how many Convolutional layers should we use, what should be the size of the filters, or the values of stride and padding? These are extremely subjective questions, and their solutions are not at all trivial in nature. No researchers have set any standard parameter to choose these hyperparameters. A neural network generally and largely depends on the type of data used for training. This data can vary in size, complexity of the input raw image, type of image processing tasks, and many other criteria. One general line of thought by looking at the big dataset, is that one has to think how to choose the hyperparameters to deduce the correct combination, which creates abstractions of the images at proper scale. We'll discuss all these in this subsection.

Depth

In the output volume, depth is considered as an important parameter. The depth corresponds to the number of filters we would like to apply for each learning iteration on some changes in the input. If the first Convolutional layer takes a raw image as the input, then multiple neurons along the depth dimension might activate in the presence of various blobs of colors or different oriented edges. The set of neurons in the same regions of input are termed as a depth column.

Stride

Stride specifies the policy of allocation of depth columns around the spatial dimension (width and height). It basically controls how the filter convolves around the input volume. Stride can be formally defined as the amount by which the filter shifts during the convolution. Ideally, the value of stride should be an integer and not a fraction. Conceptually, this amount helps in deciding how much of the input image information one wants to retain before proceeding to the next layer. The more the stride, the more information that will be retained for the next layer.

For example, when the stride is *1*, a new depth column is allocated to spatial positions, one spatial unit apart. This produces large output volumes due to heavily overlapping receptive fields in between the columns. On the other hand, if the value of stride is increased, there will be less overlapping among the receptive fields, which results in spatially smaller dimensional output volume.

We will take an example to simplify the concept a bit more. Let us imagine a *7*7* input volume and a *3*3* filter (we will ignore the third dimension for the sake of simplicity), with a stride of *1*. The output volume in this case would be of dimension *5*5*, as shown in *Figure 3.7*. However, this looks somewhat straightforward. Now, with stride 2, keeping the other parameters the same, the output volume would have less dimensionality of the order *3*3*. In this case, the receptive field will shift by *2* units, and hence, the volume will shrink to a dimension of *3*3*:

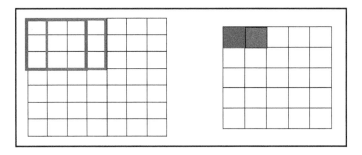

Figure 3.7: Illustration of how the filter convolves around the input volume of 7×7 with stride 1 resulting in 5×5 output volume.

This is illustrated in *Figure 3.8*. All these calculations are based on some formula mentioned in the next topic of this section. Now, if we want to increase the stride further to 3, we will have difficulties with spacing and making sure the receptive field fits on the input volume. Ideally, a programmer will raise the value of the stride only if lesser overlapping of the receptive fields is required, and if they need smaller spatial dimensions:

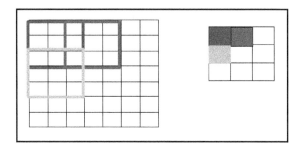

Figure 3.8: Illustration of how the filter convolves around the input volume of 7×7 with stride 2 resulting in 3×3 output volume.

Zero-padding

We've already got enough information to infer that, as we keep applying more convolution layers to the input volume, the size of the output volume decreases further. However, in some cases, we might want to preserve almost all the information about the original input volume so that we can also extract the low-level features. In such scenarios, we pad the input volume with zeroes around the borders of the input volume.

This size of zero-padding is considered as a hyperparameter. It can be defined as a hyperparameter, which is directly used to control the spatial size of the output volume in scenarios where we want to exactly preserve the spatial size of input volume.

For example, if we apply a *5*5*3* filter to a *32*32*3* input volume, the output volume will reduce to *28*28*3*. However, let's say we want to use the same Convolutional layer, but need to keep the output volume to *32*32*3*. We will use a zero-padding of size *2* to this layer. This will give us an output volume of *36*36*3*, as shown in the following figure. Now, if we apply three convolution layers with a *5*5*3* filter, it will produce an output volume of *32*32*3*, hence maintaining the exact spatial size of the input volume. *Figure 3.9* represents the pictorial views of the scenario:

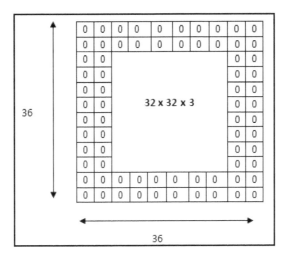

Figure 3.9: The input volume has a dimension of 32*32*3. The two borders of zeros will generate an input volume of 36*36*3. Further application of the Convolution layer, with three filters of size 5*5*3, having stride 1, will result in an output volume of 32*32*3.

Mathematical formulation of hyperparameters

This part of the chapter will introduce an equation to calculate the spatial size of the output volume based on the hyperparameters that we have discussed so far. The equation is extremely useful to choose the hyperparameter for the CNN, as these are the deciding factors to 'fit' the neurons in the network. The spatial size of the output volume can be written as a function of the input volume size (W), the receptive field size, or the filter size of the Convolutional layer neurons(K), value of the applied stride(S), and the amount of zero-padding used (P) on the border.

The equation to compute the spatial size of output volume can be written as follows:

$$O = \frac{(W - K + 2P)}{S} + 1$$

Considering the examples given in *Figure 3.7* and *Figure 3.8*, where W=7, K=3, and with no padding, P =0. For stride 1, we have S=1, and this will give the following:

$$O = \frac{(7 - 3 + 2 * 0)}{1} + 1 = 5$$

Similarly for stride **2**, the equation will give a value of **2**:

$$O = \frac{(7 - 3 + 2 * 0)}{2} + 1 = 3$$

Hence, as shown in *Figure 3.7*, we would get an output of a spatial size of **3**. However, with this configuration, when a stride of **3** is applied, it will not fit across the input volume, as this equation will return a fractional value **2.333** for the output volume:

$$O = \frac{(7 - 3 + 2 * 0)}{3} + 1 = 2.333$$

This also signifies that the values of the hyperparameter have mutual constraints. The preceding example returns a fractional value, hence, the hyperparameters would be considered as invalid. However, we might resolve the issue by adding some zero-padding around the border.

 The spatial arrangements of hyperparameters have mutual constraints.

Effect of zero-padding

As mentioned in the zero-padding section, its main purpose is to preserve the information of input volume to the next layer. To ensure same spatial size of input and output volume, the conventional formula for zero-padding, with a stride, $S=1$, is as follows:

$$P = \frac{K - 1}{2}$$

Taking the example given in *Figure 3.9*, we can verify the authenticity of the formula. In the example, $W = 32$, $K=5$, and $S=1$. Therefore, to ensure the spatial output volume to be equal to 32, we choose the number of zero-padding as follows:

$$P = \frac{5 - 1}{2} = 2$$

So, with *P=2*, the spatial size of the output volume is given as follows:

$$O = \frac{(32 - 5 + 2 * 2)}{1} + 1 = 32$$

So, this equation worked out well to preserve the same spatial dimension for the input volume and output volume.

ReLU (Rectified Linear Units) layers

In the convolution layer, the system basically computes the linear operations by doing element-wise multiplication and summations. Deep convolution usually performs the convolution operations followed by a non-linear operation after each layer. This is essential, because cascading linear operations produce another linear system. Adding non-linearity in between the layers corroborates a more expressive nature of the model than a linear model.

Therefore, after each convolution layer, an activation layer is applied on the current output. So, the main objective of this activation layer is to introduce some non-linearity to the system. Modern CNNs use **Rectified Linear Unit** (**ReLu**) as the activation function.

In artificial neural networks, the activation function, the rectifier, is defined as follows:

$$f(x) = max\ (0,\ x)$$

where *x* is the input to a neuron.

A unit operating the rectifier is termed as ReLU. Earlier, many non-linear functions such as *tan h*, sigmoid, and the like were used in the network, but in the last few years, researchers have identified that ReLU layers work much better, because they help the network to train a lot faster, without compromising the accuracy of the outcome. A significant improvement in the computational efficiency is a major factor for this.

Furthermore, this layer enhances the non-linear properties of the model and other overall networks without having any impact on the receptive fields of the Convolutional layer.

Recently, in 2013, Mass et al. [94] introduced a new version of non-linearity, termed as leaky-ReLU. Leaky-ReLU can be defined as follows:

$$Leaky\text{-}ReLU(x) = max\ (0,\ x) + \alpha\ min\ (0,\ x)$$

where $\hat{I}\pm$ is a predetermined parameter. Later, in 2015, He et al [95] updated this equation by suggesting that the parameter $\hat{I}\pm$ can also be trained, which leads to a much-improved model.

Advantages of ReLU over the sigmoid function

ReLU helps to alleviate the vanishing gradient problem, which is explained in detail in Chapter 1, *Introduction to Deep Learning*. ReLU applies the aforementioned function $f(x)$ to all the values of the input volume, and transforms all the negative activations to **0**. For max function, the gradient is defined as follows:

$$\begin{cases} 0 \text{ if } x \leq 0 \\ 1 \text{ if } x > 0 \end{cases}$$

However, for the Sigmoid function, the gradient tends to vanish as we increase or decrease the value of x.

The Sigmoid function is given as follows:

$$f(x) = \frac{1}{1 + e^{-x}}$$

The Sigmoid function has a range of [0, 1], whereas the ReLU function has the range [0, â➤➤]. Therefore, the Sigmoid function is applied to model the probability, while ReLU can be used to model all the positive numbers.

Pooling layer

This layer is the third stage of a CNN. After applying some Rectified Linear Units later, the programmer might choose to apply a Pooling layer. The layer can also be referred to as a down-sampling layer.

The pooling function is basically used to further modify the output of the layer. The primary function of the layer is to replace the output of the network at a certain location with a summarized statistics of the neighboring outputs. There are multiple options for this layer, Max-pooling being the most popular one. Max pooling operation [93] operates within a rectangular neighborhood, and reports the maximum output from it. Max-pooling basically takes a filter (generally of size 2×2) and stride of the same length, that is, **2**. The filter is then applied to the input volume, and it outputs the maximum number in every region where the filter convolves around. *Figure 3.10* shows a representation of the same thing. Other popular options for Pooling layers are the average of an *L2* normal of a rectangular neighborhood, average of a rectangular neighborhood or a weighted average, which is based on the distance from the central pixel:

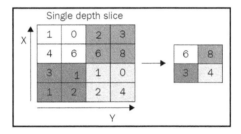

Figure 3.10: Example of Max-pool with a 2*2 filter and stride 2. Image sourced from Wikipedia.

Invariance to local translation is extremely beneficial if we are interested in the neighboring features, rather than the exact position of the feature.

Where is it useful, and where is it not?

The intuitive reason behind the Pooling layer is that once some specific feature of the original input volume is known, its exact location becomes trivial as compared to its location relative to the other features. With the help of pooling, the representation becomes almost invariant to small translations of the input. Invariance to translation signifies that for a small amount of translation on the input, the values of most of the pooled output do not vary significantly.

Invariance to local translation is extremely beneficial if we are interested in the neighboring features rather than the exact position of the feature. However, while dealing with computer vision tasks, it is required to be careful in the use of Pooling layer. Although pooling extensively helps in the reduction of complexity of the model, it might end up losing the location sensitivity of the model.

Let us take an example of image processing, which involves identifying a box in an image. Pooling layer in this case will help if we simply target to determine the existence of the box in the image. However, if the problem statement is more concerned with locating the exact position of the box, we will have to be careful enough while using the Pooling layer. As another example, let us say we are working on a language model, and are interested in identifying the contextual similarity between two words. In this case, the use of Pooling layer is not advisable, as it will lose out on some valuable feature information.

Therefore, it can be concluded that Pooling layer is basically used for reducing the computational complexity of the model. The Pooling layer is more like an averaging process, where we are more interested in a group of neighboring features. The layer can be applied in scenarios where we can afford to let go of some of the localized information.

Fully connected layer

The fully connected layer is the final layer of a CNN. The input volume for this layer comes from the output of the preceding Convolutional layer, ReLU, or Pooling layer. The fully connected layer takes this input and outputs an N dimensional vector, where N is the number of different classes present in the initial input datasets. The basic idea on which a fully connected layer works is that it works on the output received from the preceding layer, and identifies the specific feature that mostly correlates to a particular class. For example, if the model is predicting whether an image contains a cat or bird, it will have high values in the activation maps, which will represent some high-level features such as four legs or wings, respectively.

Distributed deep CNN

This section of the chapter will introduce some extremely aggressive deep CNN architecture, associated challenges for these networks, and the need of much larger distributed computing to overcome this. This section will explain how Hadoop and its YARN can provide a sufficient solution for this problem.

Most popular aggressive deep neural networks and their configurations

CNNs have shown stunning results in image recognition in recent years. However, unfortunately, they are extremely expensive to train. In the case of a sequential training process, the convolution operation takes around 95% of the total running time. With big datasets, even with low-scale distributed training, the training process takes many days to complete. The award winning CNN, AlexNet with ImageNet in 2012, took nearly an entire week to train on with two GTX 580 3 GB GPUs. The following table displays few of the most popular distributed deep CNNs with their configuration and corresponding time taken for the training process to complete:

Models	Computing power	Datasets	Number of depth	Time taken for the training process
AlexNet	Two NVIDIA GTX 580 3 GB GPUs	Trained the network on ImageNet data, which contained over 15 million high-resolution images from a total of over 22,000 categories.	eight layers	Five to six days.
ZFNet [97]	GTX 580 GPU	1.3 million images, spread over 1000 different classes.	eight layers	Twelve days.
VGG Net [98]	4 Nvidia Titan Black GPUs	The dataset includes images of 1000 classes, and is split into three sets: training (1.3 M images), validation (50 K images), and testing (100 K images with held out class labels).	19 layers	Two to three weeks.

GoogLeNet [99]	A few high-end GPUs	1.2 million images for training.	The network is 22 layers deep when counting only layers with parameters (or 27 layers if we also count pooling). The overall number of layers (independent building blocks) used for the construction of the network is about 100.	Within a week.
Microsoft ResNet [100]	8 GPU machine	Trained on the 1.28 million training images, and evaluated on the 50k validation images.	152 layers.	Two to three weeks.

Training time – major challenges associated with deep neural networks

From the preceding table, it can be surely inferred that there have been loads of efforts made by researchers to increase the accuracy of the outcome. One key point that comes out from the table is that the numbers of layers have been one of the major criteria to improve the accuracy. Microsoft's Resnet uses a neural network, as deep as 152 layers, which turns to be an extremely aggressive deep neural network. This architecture has set many new records in 2015 in classification, localization, and detection through the deep CNN. Apart from this, ResNet has also won the ILSVRC 2015 with an incredible improvement in the error rate of only 3.6%.

Although deep convolutional networks are almost about to reach the expected mark of accuracy, the major concern in almost all these deep CNNs is the rightmost column of the table. Hence, it shows that the current challenge for training deep CNNs is to build a large-scale distributed framework to parallelize the training across many CPUs and GPUs over a fast interconnected network.

Hadoop for deep CNNs

In this section, we will explain how Hadoop can be used to distribute the deep models at a large scale for faster processing.

The running times of CNNs can be divided into two major categories:

- All the Convolutional layers present in the network consume around 90-95% of the computation. They use approximately 5% of the parameters, and have large representations. [101]
- The rest of the computation, around 5-10%, is taken by the fully connected layers. They use almost 95% of the parameters, and have small representations.

Alex Krizhevsky in [101] has proposed an algorithm for training of CNN using distributed architecture. In a traditional CNN, the convolution operation itself consumes nearly the entire running time of the whole process; hence, data parallelism should be used for faster training. However, for a fully connected layer, it is advisable to use the model parallelism approach. We'll explain the algorithm using Hadoop and its YARN in this section of the chapter.

In Hadoop, the distributed system workers sit on each of the blocks of HDFS, and process the data synchronously in parallel. We will use a small batch size of 1024 numbers of examples from the raw input image, which will be split into N multiple blocks of **Hadoop Distributed File System** (**HDFS**). So, total N workers will be working for each small batch of data. The block size of HDFS would be kept as size K. Now, what should be the size of K? Although, a small size of K will increase the number of blocks and help to make the training even faster, a large number of N will also eventually increase the volume of metadata that resides in the NameNode. One major drawback in this case, is **Single Point of Failure** (**SPOF**) for Hadoop [81], which is more prone to smaller size of main memory for NameNode. However, with a bigger value of K, we will get a small number of blocks of HDFS, and hence, the number of workers working in parallel will be lesser in number. This will again make the training process slower. So, a better approach to choose the size of K will primarily depend on the following three factors:

- The availability of the primary memory's size of your NameNode.
- The size of the input batch and the complexity of operations performed on each block of data.
- How important or valuable your intermediate outcome of the data is. Based on these criteria, we can set the replication factor. However, the higher the replication factor, the higher the load of the NameNode.

The blocks of HDFS are distributed across all the DataNodes of Hadoop where YARN will operate directly on them in parallel.

The steps for distributed training of the Convolutional layer are as follows:

1. Each of the N blocks is given a different small data batch of 1024 examples from the raw input image.
2. The same size of filter and stride is applied on each of the N numbers of blocks, which results in individual spatial output based on the values of the inputs.
3. ReLU is applied on all of these, synchronously, in parallel to get some non-linearity in the outcome.
4. Max-pooling, or any other down-sampling algorithm, if desired, is applied on these separate chunks of data based on the necessity of the outcome.
5. The outputs (transformed parameters) for each iteration of the N blocks are sent back to the master-node called Resource Manager, where their parameters are averaged. The newly updated parameter is sent back to each of the N blocks to perform the actions again.
6. Steps 2 to 5 are repeated for a predefined number of epochs.

For a Fully-connected layer, one of the N number of workers working on any of the N blocks of data for a small batch of input image will send the last-stage convolutional activities to all other $(N-1)$ numbers of workers. The workers will then perform the fully-connected operation on this batch of 1024 examples, then initiate to back-propagate the gradients for these 1024 examples. The next worker, in parallel to this operation, will then send its last-stage Convolutional layer activities to the other workers similar to the earlier situation. The workers will again work on the fully-connected activities for the second batch of 1024 examples. The process will iterate until we get the outcome with the desired minimal error.

In this method, the workers broadcast their last-stage Convolutional layer's information to all other workers. The main benefit of this approach is that a large proportion $((N-1)/N)$ of the communication can be suppressed, and it can be run in parallel with the calculation of the Fully-connected layer. The approach is extremely advantageous in terms of communication of the network.

Therefore, it is very clear that Hadoop can be highly beneficial for providing a distributed environment for a CNN with the help of HDFS and Hadoop YARN.

So, now that we are familiar with the approach of distributing the model in parallel with Hadoop, the next part of the section will discuss the coding part that each of the workers will be operating on each block of HDFS.

Convolutional layer using Deeplearning4j

This section of the chapter will provide the basic idea on how to write the code for CNN using Deeplearning4j. You'll be able to learn the syntax for using the various hyperparameters mentioned in this chapter.

To implement CNN using Deeplearning4j, the whole idea can be split into three core phases: loading data or preparation of the data, network configuration, and training and evaluation of the model.

Loading data

For CNNs, generally, we only work on the image data to train the model. In Deeplearning4j, the images can be read using `ImageRecordReader`. The following code snippet shows how to load *16Ã◂16* color images for the model:

```
RecordReader imageReader = new ImageRecordReader(16, 16, false);
imageReader.initialize(new FileSplit(new
File(System.getProperty("user.home"), "image_location")));
```

After that, using `CSVRecordReader`, we can load all the image labels from the input CSV files, as follows:

```
int numLinesToSkip = 0;
String delimiter = ",";
RecordReader labelsReader = new
CSVRecordReader((numLinesToSkip,delimiter);
labelsReader.initialize(new FileSplit(new
File(System.getProperty("user.home"),"labels.csv_file_location"))
```

To combine both the images and labels data, we can use `ComposableRecordReader`. `ComposableRecordReader` can also be beneficial in cases where we need to merge data from multiple sources:

```
ComposableRecordReader(imageReader,labelsReader);
```

Similarly, instead of imageset, in some cases, if someone needs to load MNIST datasets into the model; for that, we can use the following part. This example uses a random number seed of `12345`:

```
DataSetIterator mnistTrain = new
MnistDataSetIterator(batchSize,true,12345);
DataSetIterator mnistTest = new
MnistDataSetIterator(batchSize,false,12345);
```

Model configuration

The next part of the operation is to configure the CNN. Deeplearning4j provides a simple builder to define the deep neural network layer by layer, setting the different desired hyperparameters:

```
MultiLayerConfiguration conf = new NeuralNetConfiguration.Builder()
MultiLayerConfiguration.Builder builder = new
NeuralNetConfiguration.Builder()
.seed(seed)
.iterations(iterations)
.regularization(true)
.l2(0.0005)
.learningRate(0.01)
```

The first layer, Convolutional layer, can be called using the `ConvolutionLayer.Builder` method. The `.build()` function is used to build the layer. `.stride()` is used to set the amount of stride for this Convolutional layer:

```
.layer(0, new ConvolutionLayer.Builder(5, 5)
```

`nIn` and `nOut` signify the depth. `nIn` here is `nChannels`, and `nOut` is the number of filters to be applied for the convolution:

```
.nIn(nChannels)
.stride(1, 1)
.nOut(20)
```

To add the identity function as the activation function, we will define it in this way:

```
.activation("identity")
.build())
```

To add a Pooling layer of type Max-pooling, we will call the
`SubsamplingLayer.Builder()` method after the first layer:

```
.layer(1, new SubsamplingLayer.Builder(SubsamplingLayer.PoolingType
.MAX)
.kernelSize(2,2)
.stride(2,2)
.build())
```

The **Rectifier Linear Unit (ReLU)** layer can be added by calling new
`DenseLayer.Builder().activation("relu")`:

```
.layer(4, new DenseLayer.Builder().activation("relu")
.nOut(500).build())
```

The model can be initialized by calling the `init()` method as follows:

```
MultiLayerNetwork model = new MultiLayerNetwork(getConfiguration());
model.init();
```

Training and evaluation

As mentioned in the earlier section, for the training part, we need to divide the whole big
dataset into a number of batches. The model will then work on those batches one by one in
Hadoop. Let's say we divide the dataset into 5,000 batches, each batch of size 1024
examples. The 1024 examples will then split into multiple numbers of blocks where the
workers will work in parallel. The split operation of the big dataset is done using the
`RecordReaderDataSetIterator()` method. Let's first initialize the parameters needed to
call the method as follows:

```
int batchSize = 1024;
int seed = 123;
int labelIndex = 4;
int iterations = 1
```

Let the total number of classes in the image be `10`:

```
int numClasses = 10;
```

Now, as we have set the number of parameters for `RecordReaderDataSetIterator()`, we can call the method to set up the training platform:

```
DataSetIterator iterator = new
RecordReaderDataSetIterator(recordReader,batchSize,labelIndex,numClasses);
DataSet batchData= iterator.next();
batchData.shuffle();
```

In the training phase, we can randomly split the batch into train and test datasets. If we want 70 samples for the training set and the rest 30 for the test set, we can set this configuration by using the following:

```
SplitTestAndTrain testAndTrain = batchData.splitTestAndTrain(0.70);
DataSet trainingData = testAndTrain.getTrain();
DataSet testData = testAndTrain.getTest();
trainAndTest =batchData.splitTestAndTrain(0.70);
trainInput = trainAndTest.getTrain();

testInput.add(trainAndTest.getTest().getFeatureMatrix());
```

When the model is fully trained, for each batch, the test data can be saved so as to validate the model. Hence, by defining only one object of the `Evaluation` class, we will be able to collect the statistics of the entire dataset:

```
Evaluation eval = new Evaluation(numOfClasses);
for (int i = 0; i < testInput.size(); i++)
{
    INDArray output = model.output(testInput.get(i));
    eval.eval(testLabels.get(i), output);
}
```

The model is now completely ready to be trained. This can be done by calling the `fit()` method as follows:

```
model.fit(trainInput);
```

Summary

CNNs, although not a new concept, has gained immense popularity in the last half a decade. The network primarily finds its application in the field of vision. The last few years have seen some major research on CNN by various technological companies such as Google, Microsoft, Apple, and the like, and also from various eminent researchers. Starting from the beginning, this chapter talked about the concept of convolution, which is the backbone of this type of network. Going forward, the chapter introduced the various layers of this network. Then it provided in-depth explanations for every associated layer of the deep CNN. After that, the various hyperparameters and their relations with the network were explained, both theoretically and mathematically. Later, the chapter talked about the approach of how to distribute the deep CNN across various machines with the help of Hadoop and its YARN. The last part discussed how to implement this network using Deeplearning4j for every worker working on each block of Hadoop.

In the next chapter, we will discuss another popular deep neural network called recurrent neural network. Recurrent neural network has recently gained immense popularity mainly for its ability to model the sequences of variable length. Till now, this network is successfully implemented in different problems such as language modeling, handwriting recognition, speech recognition, and so on.

4

Recurrent Neural Network

I think the brain is essentially a computer and consciousness is like a computer program. It will cease to run when the computer is turned off. Theoretically, it could be re-created on a neural network, but that would be very difficult, as it would require all one's memories.
— Stephen Hawking

To solve every problem, people do not initiate their thinking process from scratch. Our thoughts are non-volatile, and it is persistent just like the **Read Only Memory** (**ROM**) of a computer. When we read an article, we understand the meaning of every word from our understanding of earlier words in the sentences.

Let us take a real life example to explain this context a bit more. Let us assume we want to make a classification based on the events happening at every point in a video. As we do not have the information of the earlier events of the video, it would be a cumbersome task for the traditional deep neural networks to find some distinguishing reasons to classify those. Traditional deep neural networks cannot perform this operation, and hence, it has been one of the major limitations for them.

Recurrent neural networks (**RNN**) [103] are a special type of neural network, which provides many enigmatic solutions for these difficult machine learning and deep learning problems. In the last chapter, we discussed convolutional neural networks, which is specialized in processing a set of values X (For example, an image). Similarly, RNNs are magical while processing a sequence of values, $x\,(0)$, $x\,(1)$,$x(2)$,..., $x(\tau\text{-}1)$. To start with RNNs in this chapter, let us first place this network next to convolutional neural networks so that you can get an idea of its basic functionalities, and to basically know about this network.

Convolutional neural networks can easily scale to images with large width, height, and depth. Moreover, some convolutional neural networks can also process images with variable sizes.

In contrast, recurrent networks can readily scale to long sequences; also, most of those can also process variable length sequences. To process these arbitrary sequences of inputs, RNN uses their internal memory.

RNNs generally operate on mini-batches of sequences, and contain vectors x (t) with the time-step index t ranging from 0 to $(\tau-1)$. The sequence length τ can also vary for each member of the mini-batch. This time-step index should not always refer to the time intervals in the real world, but can also point to the position inside the sequence.

A RNN, when unfolded in time, can be seen as a deep neural network with indefinite number of layers. However, compared to common deep neural networks, the basic functionalities and architecture of RNNs are somewhat different. For RNNs, the main function of the layers is to bring in memory, and not hierarchical processing. For other deep neural networks, the input is only provided in the first layer, and the output is produced at the final layer. However, in RNNs, the inputs are generally received at each time step, and the corresponding outputs are computed at those intervals. With every network iteration, fresh information is integrated into every layer, and the network can go along with this information for an indefinite number of network updates. However, during the training phase, the recurrent weights need to learn which information they should pass onwards, and what they must reject. This feature generates the primary motivation for a special form of RNN, called **Long short-term memory** (**LSTM**).

RNNs started its journey a few decades back [104], but recently, it has significantly become a popular choice for modeling sequences of variable length. As of now, RNN has been successfully implemented in various problems such as learning word embedding [105], language modelling [106] [107] [108], speech recognition [109], and online handwritten recognition [110].

In this chapter, we will discuss everything you need to know about RNN and the associated core components. We will introduce Long short-term memory later in the chapter, which is a special type of RNN.

The topic-wise organization of this chapter is as follows:

- What makes recurrent networks distinctive from others?
- Recurrent neural networks(RNNs)
- Backpropagation through time (BPTT)
- Long short-term memory (LSTM)
- Bi-directional RNNs
- Distributed deep RNNs
- RNNs with Deeplearning4j

What makes recurrent networks distinctive from others?

You might be curious to know the specialty of RNNs. This section of the chapter will discuss these things, and from the next section onwards, we will talk about the building blocks of this type of network.

From `Chapter 3`, *Convolutional Neural Network*, you have probably got a sense of the harsh limitation of convolutional networks and that their APIs are too constrained; the network can only take an input of a fixed-sized vector, and also generates a fixed-sized output. Moreover, these operations are performed through a predefined number of intermediate layers. The primary reason that makes RNNs distinctive from others is their ability to operate over long sequences of vectors, and produce different sequences of vectors as the output.

> *"If training vanilla neural nets is optimization over functions, training recurrent nets is optimization over programs"*
>
> *- Alex Lebrun*

We show different types of input-output relationships of the neural networks in *Figure 4.1* to portray the differences. We show five types of input-output relations as follows:

- **One to one**: This input-output relationship is for traditional neural network processing without the involvement of a RNN. Mostly used for image classification, where the mapping is from fixed-sized input to fixed-sized output.
- **One to many**: In this kind of relationship, the input and output maintain a one-to-many relationship. The model generates a sequence of outputs with one fixed-sized input. Often observed where the model takes an image (image captioning), and produces a sentence of words.
- **Many to one**: In this type of relationship, the model takes a sequence of inputs, and outputs one single observation. For example, in case of sentiment analysis, a sentence or reviews are provided to the model; it classifies the sentence as either a positive or negative sentiment.
- **Many to many (Variable intermedia states)**: The model receives a sequence of inputs, and a corresponding sequence of outputs are generated. In this type, the RNN reads a sentence in English, and then translates and outputs a sentence in German. Used in case of Machine Translation.

- **Many to many (Fixed number of intermedia state)**: The model receives a synced sequence of input, and generates a sequence of outputs. For example, in video classification, we might wish to classify every event of the movie.

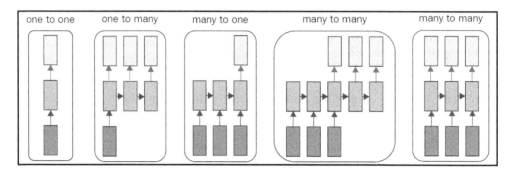

Figure 4.1: The rectangles in the figure represent each element of the sequence vector, the arrows signify the functions. Input vectors are shown in red, and output vectors are in blue. The green color represents the intermediate RNN's state. Image taken from [111].

Operations that involve sequences are generally more powerful and appealing than networks with fixed-sized inputs and outputs. These models are used to build more intelligent systems. In the next sections, we will see how RNNs are built, and how the network unites the input vectors with their state vector with a defined function to generate a new state vector.

Recurrent neural networks(RNNs)

In this section, we will discuss the architecture of the RNN. We will talk about how time is unfolded for the recurrence relation, and used to perform the computation in RNNs.

Unfolding recurrent computations

This section will explain how unfolding a recurrent relation results in sharing of parameters across a deep network structure, and converts it into a computational model.

Let us consider a simple recurrent form of a dynamical system:

$$s^{t} = f\left(s^{t-1}; \theta\right)$$

In the preceding equation, $s^{(t)}$ represents the state of the system at time t, and θ is the same parameter shared across all the iterations.

This equation is called a recurrent equation, as the computation of $s^{(t)}$ requires the value returned by $s^{(t-1)}$, the value of $s^{(t-1)}$ will require the value of $s^{(t-2)}$, and so on.

This is a simple representation of a dynamic system for understanding purpose. Let us take one more example, where the dynamic system is driven by an external signal $x^{(t)}$, and produces output $y^{(t)}$:

$$s^t = f\left(s^{t-1}, x^t; \theta\right)$$

RNNs, ideally, follow the second type of equation, where the intermediate state retains the information about the whole past sequence. However, any equation that involves recurrence can be used to model the RNN.

Therefore, similar to the feed-forward neural networks, the state of the hidden (intermediate) layers of RNNs can be defined using the variable h at time t, as follows:

$$h^t = f\left(h^{t-1}, x^t; \theta\right)$$

We will explain the functionality of this preceding equation in a RNN in the next part of this section. As of now, to illustrate the functionality of this hidden layer, *Figure 4.2* shows a simple recurrent network with no output. The left side of the figure shows a network whose current state influences the next state. The box in the middle of the loop represents the delay between two successive time steps.

As shown in the preceding recurrent equation, we can unfold or unroll the hidden states in time. The right side of the image shows the unfolded structure of the recurrent network. There, the network can be converted to a feed-forward network by unfolding over time.

In an unfolded network, each variable for each time step can be shown as a separate node of the network.

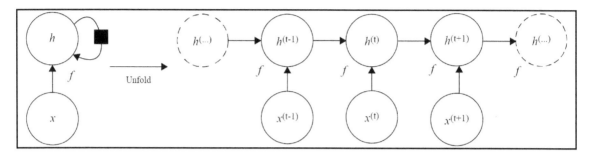

Figure 4.2: The left part of the figure shows the recurrent network where the information passes through multiple times through the hidden layer with each time step. On the right, we have the unfolded structure of the same network. Each node of this network is associated with one timestamp.

So, from *Figure 4.2*, the unfolding operation can be defined as an operation that performs the mapping of the circuit on the left-hand side to a computational model split into multiple states on the right-hand side.

Advantages of a model unfolded in time

Unfolding a network in time provides a few major advantages, which are listed as follows:

- A model without a parameter would require many training examples for learning purposes. However, learning a shared single model helps to generalize the sequence lengths, even those that are not present in the training set. This allows the model to estimate the upcoming sequence data with fewer training examples.
- Irrespective of the length of the sequence, the input size of the model will always remain the same. The input size in an unfolded model is specified in terms of transition from the hidden state to the other. However, for other cases, it is specified in terms of undefined length of the history of states.
- Due to parameter sharing, the same transition function f, with the same parameter can be used at every time step.

Memory of RNNs

As of now, you might have got some idea that the primary difference between a feed forward neural network and recurrent network is the feedback loop. The feedback loop is ingested into its own intermediate outcome as the input to the next state. The same task is performed for every element of the input sequence. Hence, the output of each hidden state depends on the previous computations. In a practical situation, each hidden state is not only concerned about the current input sequence in action, but also about what they perceived one step back in time. So, ideally, every hidden state must have all the information of the previous step's outcome.

Due to this requirement of persistent information, it is said that RNNs have their *own memory*. The sequential information is preserved as memory in the recurrent network's hidden state. This helps to handle the upcoming time steps as the network cascades forward to update the processing with each new sequence.

Figure 4.3 shows the concept of *simple recurrent neural networks* proposed by Elman back in 1990 [112]; it shows the illustration of persistent memory for a RNN.

In the next figure, a part of the word sequence AYSXWQF at the bottom represents the input example currently under consideration. Each box of this input example represents a pool of units. The forward arrow shows the complete set of trainable mapping from each sending input unit to each output unit for the next time step. The context unit, which can be considered as the persistent memory unit, preserves the output of the previous steps. The backward arrow, directed from the hidden layer to the context unit shows a copy operation of the output, used for evaluating the outcome for the next time step.

The decision where a RNN reaches at time step *t*, depends mostly on its last decision of the time step at *(t-1)*. Therefore, it can be inferred that unlike traditional neural networks, RNNs have two sources of input.

One is the current input unit under consideration, which is X in the following figure, and the other one is the information received from the recent past, which is taken from the context units in the figure. The two sources, in combination, decide the output of the current time step. More about this will be discussed in the next section.

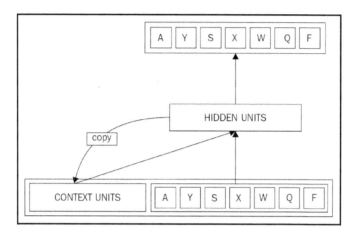

Figure 4.3: A simple recurrent neural networks with the concept of memory of RNN is shown in this figure.

Architecture

So, we have come to know that RNNs have their memory, which collects information about what has been computed so far. In this section, we will discuss the general architecture of RNNs and their functioning.

A typical RNN, unfolded (or unrolled) at the time of the calculation involved in its forward computation is shown in *Figure 4.4*.

Unrolling or unfolding a network means to write out the network for the complete sequences of input. Let us take an example before we start explaining the architecture. If we have a sequence of 10 words, the RNN would then be unfolded into a 10-layer deep neural network, one layer for each word, as depicted by the following diagram:

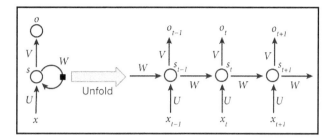

Figure 4.4: The figure shows a RNN being unrolled or unfolded into a full network.

The time period to reach from input x to output o is split into several timestamps given by *(t-1)*, *t*, *(t+1)*, and so on.

The computational steps and formulae for an RNN are listed as follows:

- In the preceding figure, x_t is the input at time step t. The figure shows computations for three timestamps *(t-1)*, *t*, and *(t+1)*, where the inputs are $x_{(t-1)}$, x_t, and $x_{(t+1)}$, respectively. For example, x_1 and x_2 are the vectors that correspond to the second and third word of the sequence.
- s_t represents the hidden state at time step t. Conceptually, this state defines the memory of the neural network. Mathematically, the formulation for s_t or the process of carrying memory can be written as follows:

$$s_t = \phi\left(Ux_t + Ws_{t-1}\right)$$

So, the hidden state is a function of the input at time step x_t, multiplied by the weight U, and addition of the hidden state of the last time step s_{t-1}, which is multiplied by its own hidden-state-to-hidden-state matrix W. This hidden-state-to-hidden-state is often termed as a transition matrix, and is similar to a Markov chain. The weight matrices behave as filters, which primarily decide the importance of both, the past hidden state and the current input. The error generated for the current state would be sent back via backpropagation to update these weights until the error is minimized to the desired value.

 To calculate the first hidden state, we would require determining the value *s-1*, which is generally initialized to all zeroes.

Unlike a traditional deep neural network, where different parameters are used for the computation at each layer, a RNN shares the same parameters (here, *U*, *V*, and *W*) across all the time steps to calculate the value of the hidden layer. This makes the life of a neural network much easier, as we need to learn fewer number of parameters.

This sum of the weight input and hidden state is squeezed by the function *f*, which usually is a nonlinearity such as a logistic sigmoid function, *tan h*, or ReLU:

- In the last figure, o_t is represented as the output at time step t. The output at step o_t is solely computed based on the memory available for the network at time t. Theoretically, although RNNs can persist memory for arbitrarily long sequences, in practice, it's a bit complicated, and they are limited to looking back only a few time steps. Mathematically, this can be represented as follows:

$$o_t = softmax\left(Vs_t\right)$$

The next section shall discuss how to train a RNN through back propagation.

Backpropagation through time (BPTT)

You have already learnt that the primary requirement of RNNs is to distinctly classify the sequential inputs. The backpropagation of error and gradient descent primarily help to perform these tasks.

In case of feed forward neural networks, backpropagation moves in the backward direction from the final error outputs, weights, and inputs of each hidden layer. Backpropagation assigns the weights responsible for generating the error, by calculating their partial derivatives: $-\delta E / \delta w$ where E denotes the error and *w* is the respective weights. The derivatives are applied on the learning rate, and the gradient decreases to update the weights so as to minimize the error rate.

However, a RNN, without using backpropagation directly, uses an extension of it, termed as **backpropagation through time** (**BPTT**). In this section, we will discuss BPTT to explain how the training works for RNNs.

Error computation

The **backpropagation through time** (**BPTT**) learning algorithm is a natural extension of the traditional backpropagation method, which computes the gradient descent on a complete unrolled neural network.

Figure 4.5 shows the errors associated with each hidden state for an unrolled RNN. Mathematically, the errors associated with each state can be given as follows:

$$E_t\left(o_t, \hat{o}_t\right) = -o_t \log \hat{o}_t$$

where o_t represents the correct output, and $\hat{o}_t$ represents the predicted word at time step t. The total error (cost function) of the whole network is calculated as the summation of all the intermediate errors at each time step.

If the RNN is unfolded into multiple time steps, starting from t_0 to t_{n-1}, the total error can be written as follows:

$$E_{total}(t_0, t_{n-1}) = \sum_{t=t_0}^{t_{n-1}} E_t(o_t, \hat{o}_t)$$

$$= -\sum_{t=t_0}^{t_{n-1}} o_t \log \hat{o}_t$$

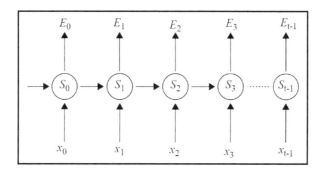

Figure 4.5: The figure shows errors associated with every time step for a RNN.

In the backpropagation through time method, unlike the traditional method, the gradient descent weight is updated in each time step.

Let w_{ij} denote the connection of weight from neuron i to neuron j. η denotes the learning rate of the network. So, mathematically, the weight update with gradient descent at every time step is given by the following equation:

$$\Delta w_{ij} = -\eta \frac{\delta E_{total}(t_0, t_{n-1})}{\delta w_{ij}}$$

$$= -\eta \sum_{t=t_0}^{t_{n-1}} \frac{\delta E_t}{\delta w_{ij}}$$

Long short-term memory

In this section, we will discuss a special unit called **Long short-term memory** (**LSTM**), which is integrated into RNN. The main purpose of LSTM is to prevent a significant problem of RNN, called the vanishing gradient problem.

Problem with deep backpropagation with time

Unlike the traditional feed forward network, due to unrolling of a RNN with narrow time steps, the feed forward network generated this way could be aggressively deep. This sometimes makes it extremely difficult to train via backpropagation through the time procedure.

In the first chapter, we discussed the vanishing gradient problem. An unfolded RNN suffers from the vanishing gradient problem of exploding while performing backpropagation through time.

Every state of a RNN depends on its input and its previous output multiplied by the current hidden state vector. The same operations happen to the gradient in the reverse direction during backpropagation through time. The layers and numerous time steps of the unfolded RNN relate to each other through multiplication, hence the derivatives are susceptible to vanish with every pass.

On the other hand, a small gradient tends to get smaller, while a large gradient gets even larger while passing through every time step. This creates the vanishing or exploding gradient problem respectively for a RNN.

Long short-term memory

In the mid-90s, an updated version of RNNs with a special unit, called **Long short-term memory** (**LSTM**) units, was proposed by German researchers Sepp Hochreiter and Juergen Schmidhuber [116] to protect against the exploding or vanishing gradient problem.

LSTM helps to maintain a constant error, which can be propagated though time and through each layer of the network. This preservation of constant error allows the unrolled recurrent networks to learn on an aggressively deep network, even unrolled by a thousand time steps. This eventually opens a channel to link the causes of effects remotely.

The architecture of LSTM maintains a constant error flow through the internal state of special memory units. The following figure (*Figure 4.6*) shows a basic block diagram of a LSTM for easy understanding:

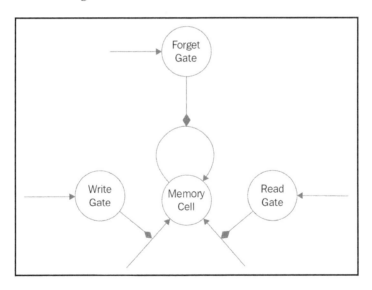

Figure 4.6: The figure shows a basic model of the Long-short term memorys

As shown in the preceding figure, an LSTM unit is composed of a memory cell that primarily stores information for long periods of time. Three specialized gate neurons– write gate, read gate, and forget gate-protect the access to this memory cell. Unlike the digital storage of computers, the gates are analog in nature, with a range of 0 to 1. Analog devices have an added advantage over digital ones, as they are differentiable, and hence, serve the purpose for the backpropagation method. The gate cell of LSTM, instead of forwarding the information as inputs to the next neurons, sets the associated weights connecting the rest of the neural network to the memory cell. The memory cell is, basically, a self-connected linear neuron. When the forget cell is reset (turned **0**), the memory cell writes its content to itself and remembers the last content of the memory. For a memory write operation though, the forget gate and write get should be set (turned **1**). Also, when the forget gate outputs something close to **1**, the memory cell effectively forgets all the previous contents that it had stored. Now, when the write gate is set, it allows any information to write into its memory cell. Similarly, when the read gate outputs a **1**, it will allow the rest of the network to read from its memory cell.

As explained earlier, the problem with computing the gradient descent for traditional RNNs is that the error gradient vanishes rapidly while propagating through the time steps in the unfolded network. Adding an LSTM unit, the error values when backpropagated from the output are collected in the memory cell of the LSTM units. This phenomenon is also known as *error carousel*. We will use the following example to describe how LSTM overcomes the vanishing gradient problem for RNNs:

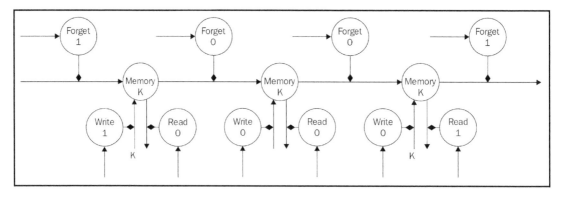

Figure 4.7: The figure shows a Long-short term memory unfolded in time. It also depicts how the content of the memory cell is protected with the help of three gates.

Figure 4.7 shows a Long short-term memory unit unrolled through time. We will start with initializing the value of the forget gate to **1** and write gate to **1**. As shown in the preceding figure, this will write an information **K** into the memory cell. After writing, this value is retained in the memory cell by setting the value of the forget gate to **0**. We then set the value of the read gate as **1**, which reads and outputs the value **K** from the memory cell. From the point of loading **K** into the memory cell to the point of reading the same from the memory cell backpropagation through time is followed.

The error derivatives received from the read point backpropagate through the network with some nominal changes, until the write point. This happens because of the linear nature of the memory neuron. Thus, with this operation, we can maintain the error derivatives over hundreds of steps without going into the trap of the vanishing gradient problems.

So there are many reasons for why Long short-term memory outperforms standard RNNs. LSTM was able to achieve the best known result in unsegmented connected handwriting recognition [117]; also, it is equally successfully applied to automated speech recognition. As of now, the major technological companies such as Apple, Microsoft, Google, Baidu, and so on have started to widely use LSTM networks as a primary component for their latest products [118].

Bi-directional RNNs

This section of the chapter will discuss the major limitations of RNNs and how bi-directional RNN, a special type of RNN helps to overcome those shortfalls. Bi-directional neural networks, apart from taking inputs from the past, takes the information from the future context for its required prediction.

Shortfalls of RNNs

The computation power of standard or unidirectional RNNs has constraints, as the current state cannot reach its future input information. In many cases, the future input information coming up later becomes extremely useful for sequence prediction. For example, in speech recognition, due to linguistic dependencies, the appropriate interpretation of the voice as a phoneme might depend on the next few spoken words. The same situation might also arise in handwriting recognition.

In some modified versions of RNN, this feature is partially attained by inserting some delay of a certain amount (N) of time steps in the output. This delay helps to capture the future information to predict the data. Although, theoretically, in order to capture most of the available future information, the value of N can be set as very large, but in a practical scenario, the prediction power of the model actually reduces with a large value of N. The paper [113] has put some logical explanation for this inference. As the value of N increases, most of the computational power of a RNN only focuses on remembering the input information for $x_{t_{c+N}}$ (from *Figure 4.8*) to predict the outcome, y_{tc}. (t_c in figure denotes the current time step in consideration). Therefore, the model will have less processing power to combine the prediction knowledge received from different input vectors. The following *Figure 4.8* shows an illustration of the amount of input information needed for different types of RNNs:

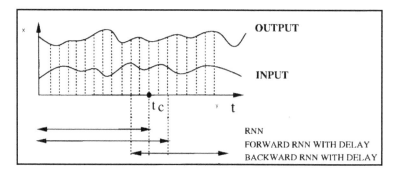

Figure 4.8: The figure shows visualizations of input information used by different types of RNNs. [113]

Solutions to overcome

To subjugate the limitations of a unidirectional RNN explained in the last section, **bidirectional recurrent network** (**BRNN**) was invented in 1997 [113].

The basic idea behind bidirectional RNN is to split the hidden state of a regular RNN into two parts. One part is responsible for the forward states (positive time direction), and the other part for the backward states (negative time direction). Outputs generated from the forward states are not connected to the inputs of the backward states, and vice versa. A simple version of a bidirectional RNN, unrolled in three time steps is shown in *Figure 4.9*.

With this structure, as both the time directions are taken care of, the currently evaluated time frame can easily use the input information from the past and the future. So, the objective function of the current output will eventually minimize, as we do not need to put further delays to include the future information. This was necessary for regular RNNs as stated in the last section.

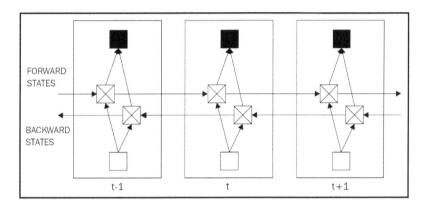

FORWARD
STATES

BACKWARD
STATES

t-1   t   t+1

Figure 4.9: The figure shows the conventional structure of a bidirectional neural network unrolled in three time steps.

So far, bidirectional RNNs have been found to be extremely useful in applications such as speech recognition [114], handwriting recognition, bioinformatics [115], and so on.

Distributed deep RNNs

As you now have an understanding of a RNN, its applications, features, and architecture, we can now move on to discuss how to use this network as distributed architecture. Distributing RNN is not an easy task, and hence, only a few researchers have worked on this in the past. Although the primary concept of data parallelism is similar for all the networks, distributing RNNs among multiple servers requires some brainstorming and a bit tedious work too.

Recently, one work from Google [119] has tried to distribute recurrent networks in many servers in a speech recognition task. In this section, we will discuss this work on distributed RNNs with the help of Hadoop.

Asynchronous stochastic gradient descent (**ASGD**) can be used for large-scale training of a RNN. ASGD has particularly shown success in sequence discriminative training of the deep neural networks.

A two-layer deep Long short-term memory RNN is used to build the Long short-term memory network. Each Long short-term memory consists of 800 memory cells. The paper uses 13 million parameters for the LSTM network. For cell input and output units tan h (hyperbolic tangent activation) is used, and for the write, read, and forget gates, the logistic sigmoid function is used.

For training purposes, the input speech training data can be split and randomly shuffled across multiple DataNodes of the Hadoop framework. The Long short-term memory is put across all these DataNodes, and distributed training is performed on those datasets in parallel. Asynchronous stochastic gradient descent is used for this distributed training. One parameter server, dedicated for maintaining the current state of all model parameters, is used.

To implement this procedure on Hadoop, each DataNode has to perform asynchronous stochastic gradient descent operations on the partitioned data. Each worker, running on each block of the DataNodes works on the partitions, one utterance at a time. For each utterance of the speech, the model parameter P is fetched from the parameter server mentioned earlier. The workers compute the current state of every frame; decipher the speech utterance to calculate the final outer gradients. The updated parameter is then sent back to the parameter server. The workers then repeatedly request the parameter server to provide the latest parameters. Backpropagation through time is then performed to calculate the updated parameter gradient for the next set of frames, which is again sent back to the parameter server.

RNNs with Deeplearning4j

Training a RNN is not a simple task, and it can be extremely computationally demanding sometimes. With long sequences of training data involving many time steps, the training, sometimes becomes extremely difficult. As of now, you have got a better theoretical understanding of how and why backpropagation through time is primarily used for training a RNN. In this section, we will consider a practical example of the use of a RNN and its implementation using Deeplearning4j.

We now take an example to give an idea of how to do the sentiment analysis of a movie review dataset using RNN. The main problem statement of this network is to take some raw text of a movie review as input, and classify that movie review as either positive or negative based on the contents present. Each word of the raw review text is converted to vectors using the Word2Vec model, and then fed into a RNN. The example uses a large-scale dataset of raw movie reviews taken from
http://ai.stanford.edu/~amaas/data/sentiment/.

The whole implementation of this model using DL4J can be split into the following few steps:

1. Download and extract the raw movie reviews data.
2. Configure the network configuration needed for training, and evaluate the performance.
3. Load each review and convert the words to vectors using the Word2Vec model.
4. Perform training for multiple predefined epochs. For each epoch, the performance is evaluated on the test set.
5. To download and extract the movie reviews' data, we need to set up the download configuration first. The following code snippet sets all the things needed to do so:

```
public static final String DATA_URL =
"http://ai.stanford.edu/~amaas/data/sentiment/*";
```

6. Location to save and extract the training and testing data in the local file path is set as follows:

```
public static final String DATA_PATH = FilenameUtils.concat
(System.getProperty("java.io.tmpdir"),local_file_path);
```

7. Location of the local filesystem for the Google News vectors is given as follows:

```
public static final String WORD_VECTORS_PATH =
"/PATH_TO_YOUR_VECTORS/GoogleNews-vectors-negative300.bin";
```

8. The following code helps to download the data from the web URL to the local file path:

```
if( !archiveFile.exists() )
{
 System.out.println("Starting data download (80MB)...");
 FileUtils.copyURLToFile(new URL(DATA_URL), archiveFile);
 System.out.println("Data (.tar.gz file) downloaded to " +
 archiveFile.getAbsolutePath());
 extractTarGz(archizePath, DATA_PATH);
}
else
{
 System.out.println("Data (.tar.gz file) already exists at " +
 archiveFile.getAbsolutePath());
 if( !extractedFile.exists())
   {
     extractTarGz(archizePath, DATA_PATH);
```

```
        }
    else
        {
            System.out.println("Data (extracted) already exists at " +
            extractedFile.getAbsolutePath());
        }
    }
}
```

9. Now, as we have downloaded the raw movie reviews' data, we can now move to set up our RNN to perform the training of this data. The downloaded data is split on a number of examples used in each mini batch to work on each worker of Hadoop for distributed training purposes. We need to declare a variable, batchSize, for this purpose. Here, as a sample, we use each batch of 50 examples, which will be split across multiple blocks of Hadoop, where the workers will run in parallel:

```
int batchSize = 50;
int vectorSize = 300;
int nEpochs = 5;
int truncateReviewsToLength = 300;
MultiLayerConfiguration conf = new
NeuralNetConfiguration.Builder()
    .optimizationAlgo(OptimizationAlgorithm.STOCHASTIC_GRADIENT_
    DESCENT)
    .iterations(1)
    .updater(Updater.RMSPROP)
    .regularization(true).l2(1e-5)
    .weightInit(WeightInit.XAVIER)
    .gradientNormalization(GradientNormalization
    .ClipElementWiseAbsoluteValue).gradientNormalizationThreshold
    (1.0)
    .learningRate(0.0018)
    .list()
    .layer(0, new GravesLSTM.Builder()
            .nIn(vectorSize)
            .nOut(200)
            .activation("softsign")
            .build())
    .layer(1, new RnnOutputLayer.Builder()
            .activation("softmax")
            .lossFunction(LossFunctions.LossFunction.MCXENT)
            .nIn(200)
            .nOut(2)
            .build())
    .pretrain(false)
    .backprop(true)
```

```
    .build();

MultiLayerNetwork net = new MultiLayerNetwork(conf);
net.init();
net.setListeners(new ScoreIterationListener(1));
```

10. As we set the network configuration for a RNN, we can now move on to the training operation as follows:

```
DataSetIterator train = new AsyncDataSetIterator(new
SentimentExampleIterator(DATA_PATH,wordVectors,
batchSize,truncateReviewsToLength,true),1);
DataSetIterator test = new AsyncDataSetIterator(new
SentimentExampleIterator(DATA_PATH,wordVectors,100,
truncateReviewsToLength,false),1);
for( int i=0; i<nEpochs; i++ )
{
  net.fit(train);
  train.reset();
  System.out.println("Epoch " + i + " complete. Starting
  evaluation:");
```

The testing of the network is performed by creating an object of the Evaluation class as follows:

```
  Evaluation evaluation = new Evaluation();
  while(test.hasNext())
  {
    DataSet t = test.next();
    INDArray features = t.getFeatureMatrix();
    INDArray lables = t.getLabels();
    INDArray inMask = t.getFeaturesMaskArray();
    INDArray outMask = t.getLabelsMaskArray();
    INDArray predicted =
    net.output(features,false,inMask,outMask);
    evaluation.evalTimeSeries(lables,predicted,outMask);
  }
test.reset();

System.out.println(evaluation.stats());
}
```

Summary

RNNs are special compared to other traditional deep neural networks because of their capability to work over long sequences of vectors, and to output different sequences of vectors. RNNs are unfolded over time to work like a feed-forward neural network. The training of RNNs is performed with backpropagation of time, which is an extension of the traditional backpropagation algorithm. A special unit of RNNs, called Long short-term memory, helps to overcome the limitations of the backpropagation of time algorithm.

We also talked about the bidirectional RNN, which is an updated version of the unidirectional RNN. Unidirectional RNNs sometimes fail to predict correctly because of lack of future input information. Later, we discussed distribution of deep RNNs and their implementation with Deeplearning4j. Asynchronous stochastic gradient descent can be used for the training of the distributed RNN. In the next chapter, we will discuss another model of deep neural network, called the Restricted Boltzmann machine.

5
Restricted Boltzmann Machines

"What I cannot create, I do not understand."
– Richard Feynman

So far in this book, we have only discussed the discriminative models. The use of these in deep learning is to model the dependencies of an unobserved variable y on an observed variable x. Mathematically, it is formulated as $P(y|x)$. In this chapter, we will discuss deep generative models to be used in deep learning.

Generative models are models, which when given some hidden parameters, can randomly generate some observable data values out of them. The model works on a joint probability distribution over label sequences and observation.

The generative models are used in machine and deep learning either as an intermediate step to generate a conditional probability density function or modeling observations directly from a probability density function.

Restricted Boltzmann machines (**RBMs**) are a popular generative model that will be discussed in this chapter. RBMs are basically probabilistic graphical models that can also be interpreted as stochastic neural networks.

Stochastic neural networks can be defined as a type of artificial neural network that is generated by providing random variations into the network. The random variation can be supplied in various ways, such as providing stochastic weights or by giving a network's neurons stochastic transfer functions.

In this chapter, we will discuss, a special type of Boltzmann machine called RBM, which is the main topic of this chapter. We will discuss how **Energy-Based models** (**EBMs**) are related to RBM, and their functionalities. Later in this chapter, we will introduce **Deep Belief network** (**DBN**), which is an extension of the RBM. The chapter will then discuss the large-scale implementation of these in distributed environments. The chapter will conclude by giving examples of RBM and DBN with Deeplearning4j.

The organization of this chapter is as follows:

- Energy-based models
- Boltzmann machine
- Restricted Boltzmann machine
- Convolutional Restricted Boltzmann machine
- Deep Belief network
- Distributed Deep Belief network
- Implementation of RBM and DBN with Deeplearning4j

Energy-based models

The main goal of deep learning and statistical modeling is to encode the dependencies between variables. By getting an idea of those dependencies, from the values of the known variables, a model can answer questions about the unknown variables.

Energy-based models (**EBMs**) [120] gather and collect the dependencies by identifying scaler energy, which generally is a measure of compatibility to each configuration of the variable. In EBMs, the predictions are made by setting the value of observed variables and finding the value of the unobserved variables, which minimize the overall energy. Learning in EBMs consists of formulating an energy function, which assigns low energies to the correct values of unobserved variables and higher energies to the incorrect ones. Energy-based learning can be treated as an alternative to probabilistic estimation for classification, decision-making, or prediction tasks.

To give a clear idea about how EBMs work, let us look at a simple example.

As shown in *Figure 5.1*, let us consider two sets of variables, observed and unobserved, namely, X and Y respectively. Variable X, in the figure, represents the collection of pixels from an image. Variable Y is discrete, and contains the possible categories of the object needed for classification. Variable Y in this case, consists of six possible values, namely: airplane, animal, human, car, truck, and none of the above. The model is used as an energy function that will measure the correctness of the mapping between X and Y.

The model uses a convention that small energy values imply highly related configuration of the variables. On the other hand, with the increasing energy values, the incompatibility of the variables also increases equally. The function that is related to both the X and Y variable is termed as energy function, denoted as follows:

$$E(Y, X)$$

In the case of energy models, the input X is collected from the surroundings and the model generates an output Y, which is more likely to answer about the observed variable X. The model is required to produce the value Y', chosen from a set Y^*, which will make the value of the energy function $E(Y, X)$ least. Mathematically, this is represented as follows:

$$Y' = argmin_{Y \in Y*} E(Y, X)$$

The following *Figure 5.1* depicts the block diagram of the overall example mentioned in the preceding section:

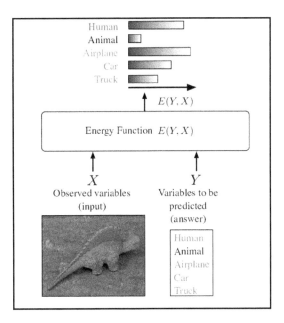

Figure 5.1: Figure shows a energy model which computes the compatibility between the observed variable X and unobserved variable Y. X in the image is a set of pixel and Y is the set of level used for categorization of X. The model finds choosing 'Animal' makes the values of energy function least. Image taken from [121]

EBMs in deep learning are related to probability. Probability is proportional to e to the power of negative energy:

$$p(x) = e^{-E(x)}$$

EBMs define probabilities indirectly by formulating the function $E(x)$. The exponential function makes sure that the probability will always be greater than zero. This also implies that in an energy-based model, one is always free to choose the energy function based on the observed and unobserved variables. Although the probabilities for a classification in an energy-based model can arbitrarily approach zero, it will never reach that.

Distribution in the form of the preceding equation is a form of Boltzmann distribution. The EBMs are hence often termed as **Boltzmann machines**. We will explain about Boltzmann machines and their various forms in the subsequent sections of this chapter.

Boltzmann machines

Boltzmann machines [122] are a network of symmetrically connected, neuron-like units, which are used for stochastic decisions on the given datasets. Initially, they were introduced to learn the probability distributions over binary vectors. Boltzmann machines possess a simple learning algorithm, which helps them to infer and reach interesting conclusions about input datasets containing binary vectors. The learning algorithm becomes very slow in networks with many layers of feature detectors; however, with one layer of feature detector at a time, learning can be much faster.

To solve a learning problem, Boltzmann machines consist of a set of binary data vectors, and update the weight on the respective connections so that the data vectors turn out to be good solutions for the optimization problem laid by the weights. The Boltzmann machine, to solve the learning problem, makes lots of small updates to these weights.

The Boltzmann machine over a d-dimensional binary vector can be defined as $x ∈ \{0, 1\}^d$. As mentioned in the earlier section, the Boltzmann machine is a type of energy-based function whose joint probability function can be defined using the energy function given as follows:

$$p(x) = \frac{\exp(-E(x))}{Z}$$

Here, $E(x)$ is the energy function and Z is termed as a partition function that confirms $Σ_x P(x)= 1$. The energy function of the Boltzmann machine is given as follows:

$$E(x) = -x^T Wx - b^T x$$

Here, W is the weight matrix of the model parameters and b is the vector of the bias parameter.

Boltzmann machines such as EBMs work on observed and unobserved variables. The Boltzmann machine works more efficiently when the observed variables are not in higher numbers. In those cases, the unobserved or hidden variables behave like hidden units of multilayer perceptron and show higher order interactions among the visible units.

Boltzmann machines have interlayer connections between the hidden layers as well as between visible units. *Figure 5.2* shows a pictorial representation of the Boltzmann machine:

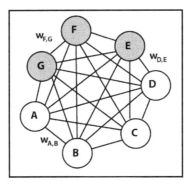

Figure 5.2: Figure shows a graphical representation of a simple Boltzmann machine. The undirected edges in the figure signifies the dependency among nodes and $w_{i,j}$ represents the weight associated between nodes i and j. Figure shows 3 hidden nodes and 4 visible nodes

An interesting property of the Boltzmann machine is that the learning rule does not change with the addition of hidden units. This eventually helps to learn the binary features to capture the higher-order structure in the input data.

The Boltzmann machine behaves as a universal approximator of probability mass function over discrete variables.

In statistical learning, **Maximize Likelihood Estimation (MLE)** is a procedure of finding the parameters of a statistical model given observations, by finding the value of one or more parameters, which maximizes the likelihood of making the observations with the parameters.

How Boltzmann machines learn

The learning algorithms for Boltzmann machines are generally based on maximum likelihood estimation method. When Boltzmann machines are trained with learning rules based on maximum likelihood estimation, the update of a particular weight connecting two units of the model will depend on only those two units concerned. The other units of the network take part in modifying the statistics that get generated. Therefore, the weight can be updated without letting the rest of the network know. In other words, the rest of the network can only know the final statistics, but would not know how the statistics are computed.

Shortfall

In Boltzmann machines, with many hidden layers, the network becomes extremely large. This makes the model typically slow. The Boltzmann machine stops learning with large scale data, as the machine's size also simultaneously grows exponentially. With a large network, the weights are generally very large and also the equilibrium distribution becomes very high. This unfortunately creates a significant problem for Boltzmann machines, which eventually results in a longer time duration to reach to an equilibrium state of distribution.

This limitation can be overcome by restricting the connectivity between two layers, and thus simplifying the learning algorithm by learning one latent layer at a time.

Restricted Boltzmann machine

The **Restricted Boltzmann machine** (**RBM**) is a classic example of building blocks of deep probabilistic models that are used for deep learning. The RBM itself is not a deep model but can be used as a building block to form other deep models. In fact, RBMs are undirected probabilistic graphical models that consist of a layer of observed variables and a single layer of hidden variables, which may be used to learn the representation for the input. In this section, we will explain how the RBM can be used to build many deeper models.

Let us consider two examples to see the use case of RBM. RBM primarily operates on a binary version of factor analysis. Let us say we have a restaurant, and want to ask our customer to rate the food on a scale of 0 to 5. In the traditional approach, we will try to explain each food item and customer in terms of the variable's hidden factors. For example, foods such as pasta and lasagne will have a strong association with the Italian factors. RBM, on the other hand, works on a different approach. Instead of asking each customer to rate the food items on a continuous scale, they simply mention whether they like it or not, and then RBM will try to infer various latent factors, which can help to explain the activation of food choices of each customer.

Another example could be to guess someone's movie choice based on the genre the person likes. Say Mr. X has supplied his five binary preferences on the set of movies given. The job of the RBM will be to activate his preferences based on the hidden units. So, in this case, the five movies will send messages to all the hidden units, asking them to update themselves. The RBM will then activate the hidden units with high probability based on some preferences given to the person earlier.

The basic architecture

The RBM is a shallow, two-layer neural network used as a building block to create deep models. The first layer of the RBM is called the observed or visible layer, the second layer is called the latent or hidden layer. It is a bipartite graph, with no interconnection allowed between any variables in the observed layer, or between any units in the latent layer. As shown in *Figure 5.3*, there is no intra-layer communication between the layers. Due to this restriction, the model is termed as a **Restricted Boltzmann machine**. Each node is used for computation that processed the input, and participated in the output by making stochastic (randomly determined) decisions about whether to convey that input or not.

 A bipartite graph is a graph wherein the vertices can be split into two disjoint sets so that every edge connects a vertex of one set to the other. However, there is no connection between the vertices of the same set. The vertex sets are usually termed as a part of the graph.

The primary intuition behind the two layers of an RBM is that there are some visible random variables (for example, food reviews from different customers) and some latent variables (such as cuisines, nationality of the customers or other internal factors), and the task of training the RBM is to find the probability of how these two sets of variables are interconnected to each other.

To mathematically formulate the energy function of an RBM, let's denote the observed layer that consists of a set of n_v binary variables collectively with the vector v. The hidden or latent layers of n_h binary random variables are denoted as h.

Similar to the Boltzmann machine, the RBM is also an energy-based model, where the joint probability distribution is determined by its energy function:

$$P(v,h) = \frac{\exp\left(-E\left(v,h\right)\right)}{Z}$$

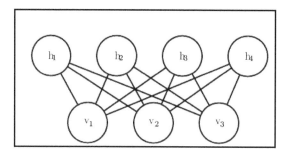

Figure 5.3: Figure shows a simple RBM. The model is a symmetric bipartite graph, where each hidden node is connected to every visible nodes. Hidden units are represented as h_i and visible units as v_i

The energy function of an RBM with binary visible and latent units is as follows:

$$E\left(v,h\right) = -a^T v - b^T h - v^T W h$$

Here, a, b, and W are unconstrained, learnable, real-valued parameters. From the preceding *Figure 5.3*, we can see that the model is split into two groups of variables, v and h. The interaction between the units is described by the matrix W.

How RBMs work

So, as we are now aware of the basic architecture of an RBM, in this section, we will discuss the basic working procedure for this model. The RBM is fed with a dataset from which it should learn. Each visible node of the model receives a low-level feature from an item of the dataset. For example, for a gray-scale image, the lowest level item would be one pixel value of the image, which the visible node would receive. Therefore, if an image dataset has n number of pixels, the neural network processing them must also possess n input nodes on the visible layer:

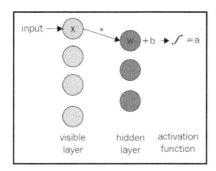

Figure 5.4 : Figure shows the computation of an RBM for a one input path

Now, let's propagate one single pixel value, *p* through the two-layer network. At the first node of the hidden layer, *p* is multiplied by a weight *w*, and added to the bias. The final result is then fed into an activation function that generates the output of the node. The operation produces the outcome, which can be termed as the strength of the signal passing through that node, given an input pixel *p*. *Figure 5.4* shows the visual representation of the computation involved for a single input RBM.

$$activation\ f((weight\ w\ *\ input\ p) + bias\ b\ ) = output\ a$$

Every visible node of the RBM is associated with a separate weight. Inputs from various units get combined at one hidden node. Each *p* (pixel) from the input is multiplied by a separate weight associated with it. The products are summed up and added to a bias. This result is passed through an activation function to generate the output of the node. The following *Figure 5.5* shows the visual representation of the computation involved for multiple inputs to the visible layer of RBMs:

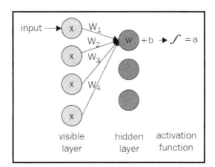

Figure 5.5: Figure shows the computation of an RBM with multiple inputs and one hidden unit

The preceding *Figure 5.5* shows how the weight associated with every visible node is used to compute the final outcome from a hidden node.

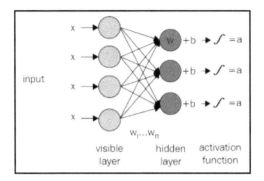

Figure 5.6: Figure shows the computation involved with multiple visible units and hidden units for an RBM

As mentioned earlier, RBMs are similar to a bipartitone graph. Further, the machine's structure is basically similar to a symmetrical bipartite graph because input received from all the visible nodes are being passed to all the latent nodes of the RBM.

For every hidden node, each input p gets multiplied with its respective weight w. Therefore, for a single input p and m number of hidden units, the input would have m weights associated with it. In *Figure 5.6*, the input p would have three weights, making a total of 12 weights altogether: four input nodes from the visible layer and three hidden nodes in the next layer. All the weights associated between the two layers form a matrix, where the rows are equal to the visible nodes, and the columns are equal to the hidden units. In the preceding figure, each hidden node of the second layer accepts the four inputs multiplied by their respective weights. The final sum of the products is then again added to a bias. This result is then passed through an activation algorithm to produce one output for each hidden layer. *Figure 5.6* represents the overall computations that occur in such scenarios.

With a stacked RBM, it will form a deeper layer neural network, where the output of the first hidden layer would be passed to the next hidden layer as input. This will be propagated through as many hidden layers as one uses to reach the desired classifying layer. In the subsequent section, we will explain how to use an RBM as deep neural networks.

Convolutional Restricted Boltzmann machines

Very high dimensional inputs, such as images or videos, put immense stress on the memory, computation, and operational requirements of traditional machine learning models. In Chapter 3, *Convolutional Neural Network*, we have shown how replacing the matrix multiplication by discrete convolutional operations with small kernel resolves these problems. Going forward, Desjardins and Bengio [123] have shown that this approach also works fine when applied to RBMs. In this section, we will discuss the functionalities of this model.

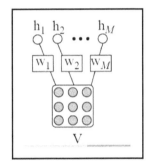

Figure 5.7 : Figure shows the observed variables or the visible units of an RBM can be associated with mini batches of image to a compute the final result. The weight connections represents a set of filters

Further, in normal RBMs, the visible units are directly related to all the hidden variables through different parameters and weights. To describe an image in terms of spatially local features ideally needs fewer parameters, which can be generalized better. This helps in detecting and extracting the identical and local features from a high dimensional image. Therefore, using an RBM to retrieve all the global features from an image for object detection is not so encouraging, especially for high dimensional images. One simple approach is to train the RBM on mini batches sampled from the input image, placed in blocks on Hadoop's Datanodes to generate the local features. The representation of this approach, termed as patch-based RBM is shown in *Figure 5.7*. This, however, has some potential limitations. The patch-based RBM, used in the distributed environment on Hadoop, does not follow the spatial relationship of mini batches, and sees each image's mini batches as independent patches from the nearby patches. This makes the feature extracted from the neighboring patches independent and somewhat significantly redundant.

To handle such a situation, a **Convolutional Restricted Boltzmann machine** (**CRBM**) is used, which is an extension of the traditional RBM model. The CRBM is structurally almost similar to RBM, a two-layer model in which the visible and hidden random variables are structured as matrices. Hence, in CRBM, the locality and neighborhood can be defined for both visible and hidden units. In CRBM, the visible matrix represents the image and the small windows of the matrix define the mini batches of the image. The hidden units of CRBM are partitioned into different feature maps to locate the presence of multiple features at multiple positions of the visible units. Units within a feature map represent the same feature at different locations of the visible unit. The hidden-visible connections of CRBM are completely local, and weights are generally split across the clusters of hidden units.

The CRBM's hidden units are used to extract features from the overlapping mini batches of visible units. Moreover, the features of neighboring mini batches complement each other and collaborate to model the input image.

Figure 5.8 shows a CRBM with a matrix of visible units **V** and a matrix of hidden units **H**, which are connected with *K* 3*3 filters, namely, $\mathbf{W}_1, \mathbf{W}_2, \mathbf{W}_3, \ldots \mathbf{W}_K$. The hidden units in the figure are split into **K** submatrices called feature map, $\mathbf{H}_1, \mathbf{H}_2, \ldots \mathbf{H}_K$. Each hidden unit $\mathbf{H}_i$ signifies the presence of a particular feature at a 3*3 neighborhood of visible units.

A CRBM, unlike a patch-based RBM, is trained on the whole input image or a large region of the image, to learn the local features and exploit the spatial relationship of the overlapping mini batches, processed in a distributed manner on Hadoop. The hidden units of overlapping mini batches depend and cooperate with each other in a CRBM. Therefore, one hidden unit, once explained, does not need to be explained again in the neighborhood overlapping mini batch. This in turn helps in reducing the redundancy of the features.

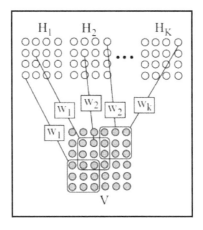

Figure 5.8: The computation involved in a CRBM is shown in the figure

Stacked Convolutional Restricted Boltzmann machines

CRBMs can be stacked together to form deep neural networks. **Stacked Convolutional Restricted Boltzmann machines** (**Stacked CRBMs**) can be trained layer wise, with a bottom-up approach, similar to the layer wise training of fully connected neural networks. After each CRBM filtering layer, in a stacked network, a deterministic subsampling method is implemented. For subsampling the features, max-pooling is performed in non-overlapping image regions. The pooling layer, as explained in `Chapter 3`, *Convolutional Neural Network*, helps to minimize the dimensionality of the features. On top of that, it makes the feature robust to small shifts and helps to propagate the higher-level feature to grow over regions of the input image.

Deep CRBMs require a pooling operation, so that the spatial size of each successive layer decreases. Although, most of the traditional convolutional models work fine with inputs of a variety of spatial size, for Boltzmann machines it becomes somewhat difficult to change the input sizes, mainly due to a couple of reasons. Firstly, the partition function of the energy function changes with the size of input. Secondly, convolutional networks attain the size invariance by increasing the size of the pooling function proportional to the input size. However, scaling the pooling regions for Boltzmann machines is very difficult to achieve.

For CRBMs, the pixels residing at the boundary of the image also impose difficulty, which is worsened by the fact that Boltzmann machines are symmetric in nature. This can be nullified by implicitly zero-padding the input. Bear in mind that, zero-padding the input is often driven by lesser input pixels, which may not be activated when needed.

Deep Belief networks

Deep Belief networks (**DBNs**) were one of the most popular, non-convolutional models that could be successfully deployed as deep neural networks in the year 2006-07 [124] [125]. The renaissance of deep learning probably started from the invention of DBNs back in 2006. Before the introduction of DBNs, it was very difficult to optimize the deep models. By outperforming the **Support Vector machines** (**SVMs**), DBNs had shown that deep models can be really successful; although, compared to the other generative or unsupervised learning algorithms, the popularity of DBNs has fallen a bit, and is rarely used these days. However, they still play a very important role in the history of deep learning.

A DBN with only one hidden layer is just an RBM.

DBNs are generative models composed of more than one layer of hidden variables. The hidden variables are generally binary in nature; however the visible units might consist of binary or real values. In DBNs, every unit of each layer is connected to every other unit of its neighbouring layer, although, there can be a DBN with sparsely connected units. There possess no connection between the intermediate layers. As shown in *Figure 5.9*, DBNs are basically a multilayer network composed of several RBMs. The connections between the top two layers are undirected. However, the connections between all other layers are directed, where the arrows point toward the layer nearest to the data.

Except for the first and last layer of the stack, each layer of a DBN serves two purposes. First, it acts as a hidden layer for its predecessor layer, and as a visible layer or input for its next layer. DBNs are mainly used to cluster, recognize and generate video sequences and images.

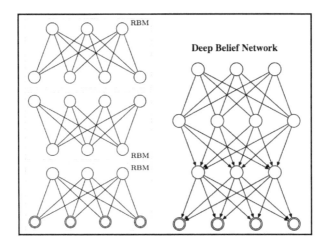

Figure 5.9: A DBN composed of three RBMs is shown in figure

Greedy layer-wise training

A greedy layer-wise training algorithm for training DBNs was proposed in 2006 [126]. This algorithm trains the DBN one layer at a time. In this approach, an RBM is first trained, which takes the actual data as input and models it.

A one-level DBN is an RBM. The core philosophy of greedy layer-wise approach is that after training the top-level RBM of an m-level DBN, the interpretation of the parameters changes while adding them in a (*m+1*) level DBN. In an RBM, between layers (*m-1*) and *m*, the probability distribution of layer *m* is defined in terms of the parameters of that RBM. However, in the case of a DBN, the probability distribution of layer *m* is defined in terms of the upper layer's parameters. This procedure can be repeated indefinitely, to connect with as many layers of DBNs as one desires.

Distributed Deep Belief network

DBNs have so far achieved a lot in numerous applications such as speech and phone recognition [127], information retrieval [128], human motion modelling[129], and so on. However, the sequential implementation for both RBM and DBNs come with various limitations. With a large-scale dataset, the models show various shortcomings in their applications due to the long, time consuming computation involved, memory demanding nature of the algorithms, and so on. To work with Big data, RBMs and DBNs require distributed computing to provide scalable, coherent and efficient learning.

To make DBNs acquiescent to the large-scale dataset stored on a cluster of computers, DBNs should acquire a distributed learning approach with Hadoop and Map-Reduce. The paper in [130] has shown a key-value pair approach for each level of an RBM, where the pre-training is accomplished with layer-wise, in a distributed environment in Map-Reduce framework. The learning is performed on Hadoop by an iterative computing method for the training RBM. Therefore, the distributed training of DBNs is achieved by stacking multiple RBMs.

Distributed training of Restricted Boltzmann machines

As mentioned in the earlier sections, the energy function for an RBM is given by:

$$E(v, h) = -a^T v - b^T h - v^T W h$$

Let an input dataset $I = \{x_i = i = 1, 2,... N\}$ be used for the distributed learning of a RBM. As discussed in the earlier section, for the learning of a DBN, the weights and biases in each level of the RBM are initialized at first by using a greedy layer-wise unsupervised training. The purpose of the distributed training is to learn the weights and the associated biases b and c. For a distributed RBM using Map-Reduce, the one Map-Reduce job is essential in every epoch.

For matrix-matrix multiplication, Gibbs sampling is used, and for training of RBMs it takes most of the computation time. Therefore, to truncate the computation time for this, Gibbs sampling can be distributed in the map phase among multiple datasets running different Datanodes on the Hadoop framework.

 Gibbs sampling is a **Markov chain Monte Carlo** (**MCMC**) algorithm for determining the sequence of observations that are estimated from a specified multivariate probability distribution, when traditional direct sampling becomes difficult.

Initially, different parameters needed for training, such as the number of neurons for visible and hidden layers, the input layer bias a, the hidden layer bias b, weight W, number of epochs (say N), learning rate, and so on, are initialized. The number of epochs signify that both the map and reduce phase will iterate for N number of times. For each epoch, the mapper runs for each block of the Datanodes, and performs Gibbs sampling to calculate the approximate gradients of W, a, and b. The reducer then updates those parameters with the computed increments needed for the next epoch. Hence, from the second epoch, the input value for the map phase, the updated values of W, a, and b, are calculated from the output of the reducer in the previous epoch.

The input dataset I is split into a number of chunks, and stored in different blocks, running on each Datanode. Each mapper running on the blocks will compute the approximate gradient of the weights and biases for a particular chunk stored on that block. The reducers then calculate the increments of respective parameters and update them accordingly. The process treats the resulting parameters and the updated values as the final outcome of the Map-Reduce phase of that particular epoch. After every epoch, the reducer decides whether to store the learned weight, if it is the final epoch or whether to increment the epoch index and propagate the key-value pair value to the next mapper.

Distributed training of Deep Belief networks

For distributed training of DBNs with L number of hidden layers, the learning is performed with pre-training L RBMs. The bottom level RBM is trained as discussed, however, for the rest of the $(L-1)$ RBMs, the input dataset is changed for each level.

The input data for m_{th} level ($L \geq m > 1$) RBM will be the conditional probability of hidden nodes of $(m-1)_{th}$ level RBMs:

$$\begin{cases} P(h1|x), when\ m = 2 \\ P(h_m|h_{m-1}, when\ L \geq m > 2 \end{cases}$$

Distributed back propagation algorithm

This is the second phase of distributed training of back propagation algorithm to tune the global network. In this procedure, while computing the gradient of weights, the feed-forward and back-propagation methods take up the majority of the computation time. Hence, for each epoch, for faster execution, this procedure should be run in parallel on each mini-batch of the input dataset.

In the first step of the procedure, the learned weights for a L level DBN, namely, $W1$, $W2,...WL$ are loaded into the memory, and other hyper-parameters are initialized. In this fine-tuning phase, the primary jobs for map and reduce phase are similar to that of the RBMs distributed training. The mapper will determine the gradients of the weights and eventually update the weight increment. The reducer updates the weight increments from one or more weights and passes the output to the mapper to perform the next iteration.

The main purpose of this procedure is to obtain some discriminative power of the model by placing the label layer on top of the global network and tuning the weights of the entire layers iteratively.

Performance evaluation of RBMs and DBNs

The paper [130] performed an experiment of distributed RBM and DBN on Hadoop cluster to provide a comparative study with the traditional sequential approach. The experiments were carried out on MNIST datasets for hand-written digits recognition. There were 60,000 images for the training set, and 10,000 images for the testing set. The block size of HDFS is set to 64 MB with a replication factor of 4. All the nodes are set to run 26 mappers and 4 reducers maximum. Interested readers can modify the block size and replication factor to see the final results of the experiments with these parameters.

Drastic improvement in training time

The purpose of this experiment is to the compare the distributed RBMs and DBNs with the traditional training policy (sequential) in terms of training time. The sequential programs were performed on one CPU, whereas the distributed programs were on 16 CPUs of a node. Both the experiments were performed on the MNIST datasets mentioned earlier. The results obtained are summarized in *Table 5.1* and *Table 5.2*:

Model	Training time
Traditional RBM	6:44 hours
Distributed RBM	1:13 hours

Table 5.1:The table represents the time needed to complete the training of distributed and sequential RBMs

Model	Training time
Traditional DBN	31:04 hours
Distributed DBN	10:35 hours

Table 5.2:The table represents the time needed to complete the training of distributed and sequential DBNs

The data shown in the table clearly depicts the advantages of using distributed RBMs and DBNs using Hadoop, over the traditional sequential approach. The training time for the distributed approach for the models has shown drastic improvement over the sequential one. Also, one crucial advantage of using the Hadoop framework for distribution is that it scales exceptionally well with the size of the training datasets, as well as the number of machines used to distribute it.

The next section of the chapter will demonstrate the programming approach for both the models using Deeplearning4j.

Implementation using Deeplearning4j

This section of the chapter will provide a basic idea of how to write the code for RBMs and DBNs using Deeplearning4j. Readers will be able to learn the syntax for using the various hyperparameters mentioned in this chapter.

To implement RBMs and DBNs using Deeplearning4j, the whole idea is very simple. The overall implementation can be split into three core phases: loading data or preparation of the data, network configuration, and training and evaluation of the model.

In this section, we will first discuss RBMs on IrisDataSet, and then we will come to the implementation of DBNs.

Restricted Boltzmann machines

For the building and training of RBMs, first we need to define and initialize the hyperparameter needed for the model:

```
Nd4j.MAX_SLICES_TO_PRINT = -1;
Nd4j.MAX_ELEMENTS_PER_SLICE = -1;
Nd4j.ENFORCE_NUMERICAL_STABILITY = true;
final int numRows = 4;
final int numColumns = 1;
int outputNum = 10;
int numSamples = 150;
```

The batchsize here can be initialized as 150, which means 150 samples of the dataset will be submitted to the Hadoop framework at a time. Rest assured all other parameters are initialized just as we did it in the earlier chapters.

```
int batchSize = 150;
int iterations = 100;
int seed = 123;
int listenerFreq = iterations/2;
```

In the next phase, the Irisdataset is loaded into the system based on the defined batchsize and number of samples per batch:

```
log.info("Load data....");
DataSetIterator iter = new IrisDataSetIterator(batchSize, numSamples);
DataSet iris = iter.next();
```

Here, the RBM is created as a layer using `NeuralNetConfiguration.Builder()`. Similarly, the object of Restricted Boltzmann is used to store properties such as the transforms applied to the observed and hidden layer – Gaussian and Rectified Linear Transforms, respectively:

```
NeuralNetConfiguration conf = new NeuralNetConfiguration.Builder()
.regularization(true)
  .miniBatch(true)
  .layer(new RBM.Builder().l2(1e-1).l1(1e-3)
    .nIn(numRows * numColumns)
    .nOut(outputNum)
```

`ReLU` is used for activation function:

```
    .activation("relu")
```

`weightInit()` function is used for initialization of the weight, which represents the starting value of the coefficients needed to amplify the input signal coming into each node:

```
    .weightInit(WeightInit.RELU)
    .lossFunction(LossFunctions.LossFunction.RECONSTRUCTION
    _CROSSENTROPY.k(3)
```

Gaussian Transformation is used for visible units and Rectified Linear Transformation is used for hidden layers. This is very simple in Deeplearning4j. We need to pass the parameters `VisibleUnit.GAUSSIAN` and `HiddenUnit.RECTIFIED` inside the `.visibleUnit` and `.hiddenUnit` methods:

```
    .hiddenUnit(HiddenUnit.RECTIFIED).visibleUnit(VisibleUnit.GAUSSIAN)
    .updater(Updater.ADAGRAD).gradientNormalization(Gradient
     Normalization.ClipL2PerLayer)
    .build())
  .seed(seed)
  .iterations(iterations)
```

The Backpropagation step size is defined here:

```
    .learningRate(1e-3)
    .optimizationAlgo(OptimizationAlgorithm.LBFGS)
    .build();
Layer model = LayerFactories.getFactory(conf.getLayer()).create(conf);
model.setListeners(new ScoreIterationListener(listenerFreq));
log.info("Evaluate weights....");
INDArray w = model.getParam(DefaultParamInitializer.WEIGHT_KEY);
log.info("Weights: " + w);
```

To scale to dataset, `scale()` can be called with the object of the Dataset class:

```
iris.scale();
```

After the evaluation was done in the earlier process, the model is now completely ready to be trained. It can be trained in a similar manner using the `fit()` method, as done for the earlier models, and passing `getFeatureMatrix` as the parameter:

```
log.info("Train model....");
for(int i = 0; i < 20; i++)
  {
   log.info("Epoch "+i+":");
   model.fit(iris.getFeatureMatrix());
  }
```

Deep Belief networks

As explained in this chapter, a DBN is a stacked version of the number of RBMs. In this part, we will show how to deploy DBNs programmatically using Deeplearning4j. The flow of the program will follow the standard procedure as with other models. The implementation of simple DBNs is pretty simple using Deeplearning4j. The example will show how to train and traverse the input MNIST data with DBNs.

For MNIST dataset, the following line specifies the batchsize and number of examples, which one user will specify to load the data in HDFS at one time:

```
log.info("Load data....");
DataSetIterator iter = new MnistDataSetIterator(batchSize,numSamples,
true);
```

In the next phase, the model will be built by stacking 10 RBMs together. The following piece of code will specify the way this should be done using Deeplearning4j:

```
log.info("Build model....");
MultiLayerConfiguration conf = new NeuralNetConfiguration.Builder()
  .seed(seed)
  .iterations(iterations)
  .optimizationAlgo(OptimizationAlgorithm.LINE_GRADIENT_DESCENT)
  .list()
  .layer(0, new RBM.Builder().nIn(numRows * numColumns).nOut(1000)
  .lossFunction(LossFunctions.LossFunction.RMSE_XENT).build())
  .layer(1, new RBM.Builder().nIn(1000).nOut(500)
  .lossFunction(LossFunctions.LossFunction.RMSE_XENT).build())
  .layer(2, new RBM.Builder().nIn(500).nOut(250)
  .lossFunction(LossFunctions.LossFunction.RMSE_XENT).build())
```

```
    .layer(3, new RBM.Builder().nIn(250).nOut(100)
    .lossFunction(LossFunctions.LossFunction.RMSE_XENT).build())
    .layer(4, new RBM.Builder().nIn(100).nOut(30)
    .lossFunction(LossFunctions.LossFunction.RMSE_XENT).build())
    .layer(5, new RBM.Builder().nIn(30).nOut(100)
    .lossFunction(LossFunctions.LossFunction.RMSE_XENT).build())
    .layer(6, new RBM.Builder().nIn(100).nOut(250)
    .lossFunction(LossFunctions.LossFunction.RMSE_XENT).build())
    .layer(7, new RBM.Builder().nIn(250).nOut(500)
    .lossFunction(LossFunctions.LossFunction.RMSE_XENT).build())
    .layer(8, new  RBM.Builder().nIn(500).nOut(1000)
    .lossFunction(LossFunctions.LossFunction.RMSE_XENT).build())
    .layer(9, new OutputLayer.Builder(LossFunctions.LossFunction.
    RMSE_XENT).nIn(1000).nOut(numRows*numColumns).build())
    .pretrain(true)
    .backprop(true)
    .build();
MultiLayerNetwork model = new MultiLayerNetwork(conf);
model.init();
```

In the last part, the code will be trained using the loaded MNIST dataset, by calling the `fit()` method:

```
log.info("Train model....");
while(iter.hasNext())
    {
    DataSet next = iter.next();
    model.fit(new DataSet(next.getFeatureMatrix(),next.
    getFeatureMatrix()));
    }
```

Upon executing the code, the process will give a following output:

```
Load data....
Build model....
Train model....


o.d.e.u.d.DeepAutoEncoderExample - Train model....
o.d.n.m.MultiLayerNetwork - Training on layer 1 with 1000 examples
o.d.o.l.ScoreIterationListener - Score at iteration 0 is 394.462
o.d.n.m.MultiLayerNetwork - Training on layer 2 with 1000 examples
o.d.o.l.ScoreIterationListener - Score at iteration 1 is 506.785
o.d.n.m.MultiLayerNetwork - Training on layer 3 with 1000 examples
o.d.o.l.ScoreIterationListener - Score at iteration 2 is 255.582
o.d.n.m.MultiLayerNetwork - Training on layer 4 with 1000 examples
o.d.o.l.ScoreIterationListener - Score at iteration 3 is 128.227
```

```
. . . . . . . . . . . . . . . . . . . . . . . . . . . . . . . . . . . .

o.d.n.m.MultiLayerNetwork - Finetune phase
o.d.o.l.ScoreIterationListener - Score at iteration 9 is 132.45428125


. . . . . . . . . . . . . . . . . . . . . . . . . . .

o.d.n.m.MultiLayerNetwork - Finetune phase
o.d.o.l.ScoreIterationListener - Score at iteration 31 is 135.949859375
o.d.o.l.ScoreIterationListener - Score at iteration 32 is 135.9501875
o.d.n.m.MultiLayerNetwork - Training on layer 1 with 1000 examples
o.d.o.l.ScoreIterationListener - Score at iteration 33 is 394.182
o.d.n.m.MultiLayerNetwork - Training on layer 2 with 1000 examples
o.d.o.l.ScoreIterationListener - Score at iteration 34 is 508.769
o.d.n.m.MultiLayerNetwork - Training on layer 3 with 1000 examples


. . . . . . . . . . . . . . . . . . . . . . . . . .

o.d.n.m.MultiLayerNetwork - Finetune phase
o.d.o.l.ScoreIterationListener - Score at iteration 658 is 142.4304375
o.d.o.l.ScoreIterationListener - Score at iteration 659 is 142.4311875
```

Summary

The RBM is a generative model, which can randomly produce visible data values when some latent or hidden parameters are supplied to it. In this chapter, we have discussed the concept and mathematical model of the Boltzmann machine, which is an energy-based model. The chapter then discusses and gives a visual representation of the RBM. Further, this chapter discusses CRBM, which is a combination of Convolution and RBMs to extract the features of high dimensional images. We then moved toward popular DBNs that are nothing but a stacked implementation of RBMs. The chapter further discusses the approach to distribute the training of RBMs as well as DBNs in the Hadoop framework.

We conclude the chapter by providing code samples for both the models. The next chapter of the book will introduce one more generative model called autoencoder and its various forms such as de-noising autoencoder, deep autoencoder, and so on.

6
Autoencoders

"People worry that computers will get too smart and take over the world, but the real problem is that they're too stupid and they've already taken over the world."
– Pedro Domingos

In the last chapter, we discussed a generative model called Restricted Boltzmann machine. In this chapter, we will introduce one more generative model called **autoencoder**. Autoencoder, a type of artificial neural network, is generally used for dimensionality reduction, feature learning, or extraction.

As we move on with this chapter, we will discuss the concept of autoencoder and its various forms in detail. We will also explain the terms *regularized autoencoder* and *sparse autoencoder*. The concept of sparse coding, and selection criteria of the sparse factor in a sparse autoencoder will be taken up. Later, we will talk about the deep learning model, deep autoencoder, and its implementation using Deeplearning4j. Denoising autoencoder is one more form of a traditional autoencoder, which will be discussed in the end part of the chapter.

Overall, this chapter is broken into a few subsections, which are listed as follows:

- Autoencoder
- Sparse autoencoder
- Deep autoencoder
- Denoising autoencoder
- Applications of autoencoders

Autoencoder

An autoencoder is a neural network with one hidden layer, which is trained to learn an identity function that attempts to reconstruct its input to its output. In other words, the autoencoder tries to copy the input data by projecting onto a lower dimensional subspace defined by the hidden nodes. The hidden layer, h, describes a code, which is used to represent the input data and its structure. This hidden layer is thus forced to learn the structure from its input training dataset so that it can copy the input at the output layer.

The network of an autoencoder can be split into two parts: encoder and decoder. The encoder is described by the function $h=f(k)$, and a decoder that tries to reconstruct or copy is defined by $r = g(h)$. The basic idea of autoencoder should be to copy only those aspects of the inputs which are prioritized, and not to create an exact replica of the input. They are designed in such a way so as to restrict the hidden layer to copy only approximately, and not everything from the input data. Therefore, an autoencoder will not be termed as useful if it learns to completely set $g(f(k)) = k$ for all the values of k. *Figure 6.1* represents the general structure of an autoencoder, mapping an input k to an output r through an internal hidden layer of code h:

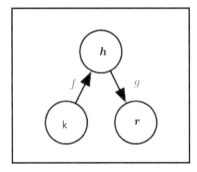

Figure 6.1: General block diagram of an autoencoder. Here, input k is mapped to an output r through a hidden state or internal representation h. An encoder f maps the input k to the hidden state h, and decoder g performs the mapping of h to the output r.

To provide one more example, let us consider *Figure 6.2*. The figure shows a practical representation of an autoencoder for input image patches k, which learns the hidden layer h to output r. The input layer k is a combination of intensity values from the image patches. The hidden layer nodes help to project the high-dimensional input layer into lower-dimensional activation values of the hidden nodes. These activation values of the hidden node are merged together to generate the output layer r, which is an approximation of the input pixel. In ideal cases, hidden layers generally have a smaller number of nodes as compared to the input layer nodes. For this reason, they are forced to diminish the information in such a way that the output layer can still be generated.

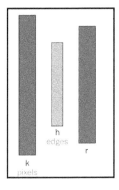

Figure 6.2: Figure shows a practical example of how an autoencoder learns output structure from the approximation of the input pixels.

Replicating the structure of the input to the output might sound inefficacious, however, practically, the final result of an autoencoder is not exactly dependent on the output of the decoder. Instead, the main idea behind training an autoencoder is to copy the useful properties of the input task, which will reflect in the hidden layer.

One of the common ways to extract desired features or information from the autoencoder is to limit the hidden layer, h, to have smaller dimension (d') than the input k with a dimension d, that is $d'<d$. This resulting smaller dimensional layer can thus be called a loss compressed representation of the input k. An autoencoder whose hidden layer's dimension is less than the input's dimension is termed as *undercomplete*.

The learning process described can be mathematically represented as minimizing the loss function L, which is given as follows:

$$L\left(k, g\left(f\left(k\right)\right)\right)$$

In simple words, L can be defined as a loss function that penalized $g\left(f\left(k\right)\right)$ for being different from the input k.

With a linear decoder function, an autoencoder learns to form the basis for space as similar to the **Principal component analysis** (**PCA**) procedure. Upon convergence, the hidden layer will form a basis for the space spanned by the principal subspace of the training dataset given as the input. However, unlike PCA, these procedures need not necessarily generate orthogonal vectors. For this reason, autoencoders with non-linear encoder functions f and non-linear decoder function g can learn more powerful non-linear generalization of the PCA. This will eventually increase the capacity of the encoder and decoder to a large extent. With this increase in capacity, however, the autoencoder starts showing unwanted behavior.

It can then learn to undergo copying the whole input without giving attention to extract the desired information. In a theoretical sense, an autoencoder might be a one-dimensional code, but practically, a very powerful nonlinear encoder can learn to represent each training example $k(i)$ with code i. The decoder then maps those integers (i) to the values of specific training examples. Hence, copying of only the useful features from the input dataset fails completely with an autoencoder with higher capacity.

 PCA is a statistical method which applies orthogonal transformation to convert a set of possibly correlated observed variables into a set of linearly correlated set of variables termed as principal components. The number of principal components in the PCA method is less than or equal to the number of original input variables.

Similar to the edge case problem mentioned for an undercomplete autoencoder, where the dimension of the hidden layer is less than that of the input, autoencoder, where the hidden layer or code is allowed to have an equal dimension of input, often faces the same problem.

An autoencoder, where the hidden code has greater dimension than the dimension of the input, is termed as an overcomplete autoencoder. This type of autoencoder is even more vulnerable to the aforementioned problems. Even a linear encoder and decoder can perform learning a copy of input to output without learning any desired attributes of the input dataset.

Regularized autoencoders

By choosing a proper dimension for the hidden layer, and the capacity of the encoder and decoder in accordance with the complexity of the model distribution, autoencoders of any kind of architecture can be built successfully. The autoencoder which has the ability to provide the same is termed as a regularized autoencoder.

Besides the ability to copy the input to output, a regularized autoencoder has a loss function, which helps the model to possess other properties too. These include robustness to missing inputs, sparsity of the representation of data, smallness of the derivative of the representation, and so on. Even a nonlinear and *overcomplete* regularized autoencoder is able to learn at least something about the data distribution, irrespective of the capacity of the model. Regularized autoencoders [131] are able to capture the structure of the training distribution with the help of productive opposition between a restructuring error and a regularizer.

Sparse autoencoders

Distributed sparse representation is one of the primary keys to learn useful features in deep learning algorithms. Not only is it a coherent mode of data representation, but it also helps to capture the generation process of most of the real world dataset. In this section, we will explain how autoencoders encourage sparsity of data. We will start with introducing sparse coding. A code is termed as sparse when an input provokes the activation of a relatively small number of nodes of a neural network, which combine to represent it in a sparse way. In deep learning technology, a similar constraint is used to generate the sparse code models to implement regular autoencoders, which are trained with sparsity constants called sparse autoencoders.

Sparse coding

Sparse coding is a type of unsupervised method to learn sets of *overcomplete* bases in order to represent the data in a coherent and efficient way. The primary goal of sparse coding is to determine a set of vectors (n) v_i such that the input vector k can be represented as a linear combination of these vectors.

Mathematically, this can be represented as follows:

$$k = \sum_{i=1}^{n} a_i v_i$$

Here a_i is the coefficient associated with each vector v_i.

With the help of PCA, we can learn a complete set of basis vectors in a coherent way; however, we want to learn an *overcomplete* set of basis vectors to represent the input vector $k \hat{a} \rightarrow \rightarrow \hat{a} \rightarrow \rightarrow^m$, where $n>m$. The reason to have the *overcomplete* basis is that the basis vectors are generally able to catch the pattern and structure that are inherent to the input data. However, overcompleteness sometime raises a degeneracy that, with its basis, the coefficient a_i cannot uniquely identify the input vector k. For this reason, an additional criterion called sparsity is introduced in sparse coding.

In a simple way, sparsity can be defined as having few non-zero components or having few components that are not close to zero. The set of coefficients a_i is termed as sparse if, for a given input vector, the number of non-zero coefficients, or the number of coefficients that are way far from zero, should be a few.

With this basic understanding of sparse coding, we can now move to the next part to discover how the sparse coding concept is used for autoencoders to generate sparse autoencoders.

Sparse autoencoders

When the input dataset maintains some structure, and if the input features are correlated, then even a simple autoencoder algorithm can discover those correlations. Moreover, in such cases, a simple autoencoder will end up learning a low-dimensional representation, which is similar to PCA.

This perception is based on the fact that the number of hidden layers is relatively small. However, by imposing other constraints on the network, even with a large number of hidden layers, the network can still discover desired features from the input vectors.

Sparse autoencoders are generally used to learn features to perform other tasks such as classification. Autoencoders for which the sparsity constraints have been added must respond to the unique statistical features of the input dataset with which it is training on, rather than simply acting as an identity function.

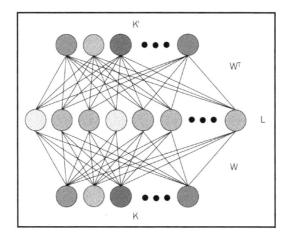

Figure 6.3: Figure shows a typical example of a sparse autoencoder

Sparse autoencoders are a type of autoencoder with a sparsity enforcer, which helps to direct a single layer network to learn the hidden layer code. This approach minimizes the reconstruction errors along with restricting the number of code words needed to restructure the output. This kind of sparsifying algorithm can be considered as a classification problem that restricts the input to a single class value, which helps to reduce the prediction errors.

In this part, we will explain sparse autoencoder with a simple architecture. *Figure 6.3* shows the simplest form of a sparse autoencoder, consisting of a single hidden layer h. The hidden layer h, is connected to the input vector K by a weight matrix, W, which forms the encoding step. In the decoder step, the hidden layer h outputs to a reconstruction vector $K`$ with the help of the tied weight matrix W^T. In the network, the activation function is denoted as f and the bias term as b. The activation function could be anything: linear, sigmoidal, or ReLU.

The equation to compute the sparse representation of the hidden code l is written as follows:

$$l = f(WK' + b)$$

The reconstructed output is the hidden representation, mapped linearly to the output using this:

$$K' = f(W^T l + b')$$

Learning occurs via backpropagation on the reconstruction error. All the parameters are optimized to minimize the mean square error, given as follows:

$$\min \left\| K' - K \right\|_2^2$$

As we have the network setup now, we can add the sparsifying component, which drives the vector L towards a sparse representation. Here, we will use k-Sparse autoencoders to implement the sparse representation of the layer. (Don't get confused between the k of k-Sparse representation and K input vector. To distinguish between both of them, we have denoted these two with a small k and capital K respectively.)

The k-Sparse autoencoder

The k-Sparse autoencoder [132] is based on an autoencoder with tied weights and linear activation functions. The basic idea of a k-Sparse autoencoder is very simple. In the feed-forward phase of the autoencoder, once we compute the hidden code $l = WK + b$, rather than reconstructing the input from all the hidden units, the method searches for the k largest hidden units and sets the remaining hidden units' values as zero.

There are alternative methods to determine the k largest hidden units. By sorting the activities of the hidden units or using ReLU, hidden units with thresholds are adjusted until we determine the k largest activities. This selection step to find the k largest activities is non-linear. The selection step behaves like a regularizer, which helps to prevent the use of large numbers of hidden units while building the output by reconstructing the input.

How to select the sparsity level k

An issue might arise during the training of a k-Sparse autoencoder if we enforce a low sparsity level, say $k=10$. One common problem is that in the first few epochs, the algorithm will aggressively start assigning the individual hidden units to groups of training cases. The phenomena can be compared with the k-means clustering approach. In the successive epochs, these hidden units will be selected and re-enforced, but the other hidden units would not be adjusted.

This issue can be addressed by scheduling the sparsity level in a proper way. Let us assume we are aiming for a sparsity level of 10. In such cases, we can start with a large sparsity level of say $k=100$ or $k=200$. Hence, the k-Sparse autoencoder can train all the hidden units present. Gradually, over half of the epoch, we can linearly decrease the sparsity level of $k=100$ to $k=10$. This greatly increases the chances of all the hidden units being picked. Then, we will keep $k=10$ for the next half of the epoch. In this way, this kind of scheduling will guarantee that even with a low sparsity level, all of the filters will be trained.

Effect of sparsity level

The choice of value of k is very much crucial while designing or implementing a k-Sparse autoencoder. The value of k determines the desirable sparsity level, which helps to make the algorithm ideal for a wide variety of datasets. For example, one application could be used to pre-train a deep discriminative neural network or a shallow network.

If we take a large value for k (say $k=200$ on an MNIST dataset), the algorithm will tend to identify and learn very local features of the dataset. These features sometimes behave too prematurely to be used for the classification of a shallow architecture. A shallow architecture generally has a naive linear classifier, which does not really have enough architectural strength to merge all of these features and achieve a substantial classification rate. However, similar local features are very much desirable to pre-train a deep neural network.

For a smaller value of the sparsity level (say *k=10* on an MNIST dataset), the output is reconstructed from the input using a smaller set of hidden units. This eventually results in detecting of global features from the datasets, instead of local features as in the earlier case. These less local features are suitable for shallow architecture for the classification tasks. On the contrary, these types of situations are not ideal for deep neural networks.

Deep autoencoders

So far, we have talked only about single-layer encoders and single-layer decoders for a simple autoencoder. However, a deep autoencoder with more than one encoder and decoder brings more advantages.

Feed-forward networks perform better when they are deep. Autoencoders are basically feed-forward networks; hence, the advantages of a basic feed-forward network can also be applied to autoencoders. The encoders and decoders are autoencoders, which also work like a feed-forward network. Hence, we can deploy the advantages of the depth of a feed-forward network in these components also.

In this context, we can also talk about the universal approximator theorem, which ensures that a feed-forward neural network with at least one hidden layer, and with enough hidden units, can produce an approximation of any arbitrary function to any degree of accuracy. Following this concept, a deep autoencoder having at least one hidden layer, and containing sufficient hidden units, can approximate any mapping from input to code arbitrarily well.

 One can approximate any continuous function to any degree of accuracy with a two-layer network. In the mathematical theory of artificial neural networks, the universal approximation function states that a feed-forward network can approximate any continuous function of a compact subset of R^n, if it has at least one hidden layer with a finite number of neurons.

Deep autoencoder provides many advantages as compared to shallow architecture. The non-trivial depth of an autoencoder suppresses the computation of representing a few functions. Also, the depth of autoencoders drastically reduces the amount of training data required to learn the functions. Even experimentally, it has been found that deep autoencoders provide better compression when compared to shallow autoencoders.

To train a deep autoencoder, the common practice is to train a stack of shallow autoencoders. Therefore, to train a deep autoencoder, a series of shallow autoencoders are encountered frequently. In the next subsections, we will discuss the concept of deep autoencoders in depth.

Training of deep autoencoders

The design of a deep autoencoder explained here is based on MNIST handwritten digit databases. In the paper [133],a well-structured procedure of building and training of a deep autoencoder is explained. The fundamentals of training a deep autoencoder is through three phases, that is: Pre-training, Unrolling, and Fine-tuning.

1. **Pre-training**: The first phase of training a deep autoencoder is 'pre-training'. The main purpose of this phase is to work on binary data, generalize in to a real-valued data, and then to conclude that it works well for various datasets.

   We already have enough insights that a single layer of hidden units is not the proper way to model the structure in a large set of images. A deep autoencoder is composed of multiple layers of a Restricted Boltzmann machine. In Chapter 5, *Restricted Boltzmann Machines* we gave enough information on how a Restricted Boltzmann machine works. Using the same concept, we can proceed to build the structure for a deep autoencoder:

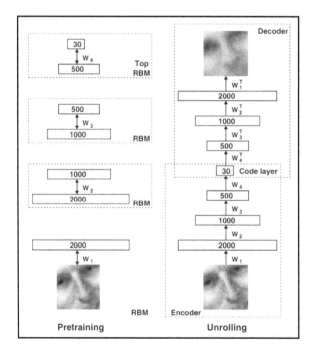

Figure 6.4: Pre-training a deep autoencoder involves learning a stack of Restricted Boltzmann machines (RBMs) where each RBM possesses a single layer of feature detectors. The learned features of one Restricted Boltzmann machine is used as the 'input data' to train the next RBM of the stack. After the pre-training phase, all the RBMs are unfolded or unrolled to build a deep autoencoder. This deep autoencoder is then fine-tuned using the backpropagation approach of error derivatives.

When the first layer of the RBM is driven by a stream of data, the layer starts to learn the feature detectors. This learning can be treated as input data for learning for the next layer. In this way, feature detectors of the first layer become the visible units for learning the next layer of the Restricted Boltzmann machine. This procedure of learning layer-by-layer can be iterated as many times as desired. This procedure is indeed very much effectual in pre-training the weights of a deep autoencoder. The features captured after each layer have a string of high-order correlations between the activities of the hidden units below. The first part of *Figure 6.4* gives a flow diagram of this procedure. Processing the benchmark dataset MNIST, a deep autoencoder would use binary transformations after each RBM. To process real-valued data, deep autoencoders use Gaussian rectified transformations after each Restricted Boltzmann machine layer.

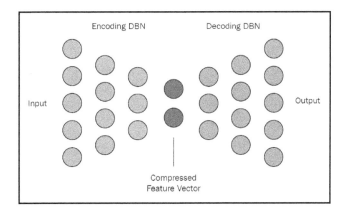

Figure 6.5: Pictorial representation of how the number or vectors of encoder and decoder varies during the phases.

2. **Unrolling**: Once the multiple layers of feature detectors of the deep autoencoders are pre-trained, the whole model is unrolled to generate the encoder and decoder networks, which at first use the same weights. We will explain each of the designs of each part given in the second part of the image separately to have a better understanding of this phase.

• **Encoder**: For an MNIST dataset of *28×28* pixel images, the input that the network will get is that of 784 pixels. As per the rule of thumb, the number of parameters of the first layer of the deep autoencoder should be slightly larger. As shown in *Figure 6.4*, **2000** parameters are taken for the first layer of the network. This might sound unreasonable, as taking more parameters as inputs increase the chance of overfitting the network. However, in this case, increasing the number of parameters will eventually increase the features of the input, which, in turn, make the decoding of the autoencoder data possible.

As shown in *Figure 6.4*, the layers would be **2000**, **1000**, **500**, and **30**-nodes wide respectively. A snapshot of this phenomenon is depicted in *Figure 6.5*. In the end, the encoder will produce a vector **30** numbers long. This **30** number vector is the last layer of the encoder of the deep autoencoder. A rough outline for this encoder will be as follows:

$$784(input) \rightarrow 2000 \rightarrow 1000 \rightarrow 500 \rightarrow 30$$

- **Decoder**: The **30** number vectors found at the end of the encoding phase are the encoded version of the 28×28 pixel images. The second part of the deep autoencoder is the decoder phase, where it basically learns how to decode the condensed vector. Hence, the output of the encoder phase (**30**-number vectors) becomes the input of the decoder phase. This half of the deep autoencoder is a feed-forward network, where the encoded condensed vector proceeds towards the reconstructed input after each layer. The layers shown in *Figure 6.4* are **30**, **500**, **1000**, and **2000**. The layers initially possess the same weights as their counterparts in the pre-training network; it is just that the weights are transposed as shown in the figure. A rough outline for this encoder will be as follows:

$$784(output) \leftarrow 2000 \leftarrow 1000 \leftarrow 500 \leftarrow 30$$

So, the main purpose of decoding half of a deep autoencoder is to learn how to reconstruct the image. The operation is carried out in the second feed-forward network that also performs back propagation, which happens through reconstruction entropy.

3. **Fine-tuning**: In the fine-tuning phase, the stochastic activities are replaced by the deterministic, real-valued probabilities. The weights associated with each layer of the whole deep autoencoder are fine-tuned for optimal reconstruction by using the backpropagation method.

Implementation of deep autoencoders using Deeplearning4j

So, you now have sufficient idea of how to build a deep autoencoder using a number of Restricted Boltzmann machines. In this section, we will explain how to design a deep autoencoder with the help of Deeplearning4j.

We will use the same MNIST dataset as in the previous section, and keep the design of the deep autoencoder similar to what we explained earlier.

As already explained in earlier examples, a small batch size of 1024 number of examples is used from the raw MNIST datasets, which can be split into *N* multiple blocks of Hadoop. These *N* multiple blocks will run on the Hadoop Distributed File System by each worker in parallel. The flow of code to implement the deep autoencoder is simple and straightforward.

The steps are shown as follows:

1. Batch-wise loading of the MNIST dataset in HDFS. Each batch will contain 1024 number of examples.
2. Start building the model.
3. Perform the encoding operation.
4. Perform the decoding operation.
5. Train the model by calling the `fit()` method.

```
final int numRows = 28;
```

Initial configuration needed to set the Hadoop environment. The `batchsize` is set to 1024.

```
final int numColumns = 28;
int seed = 123;
int numSamples = MnistDataFetcher.NUM_EXAMPLES;
int batchSize = 1024;
int iterations = 1;
int listenerFreq = iterations/5;
```

Load the data into the HDFS:

```
log.info("Load data....");
DataSetIterator iter = new
MnistDataSetIterator(batchSize,numSamples,true);
```

We are now all set to build the model to add the number of layers of the Restricted Boltzmann machine to build the deep autoencoder:

```
log.info("Build model....");
MultiLayerConfiguration conf = new NeuralNetConfiguration.Builder()
    .seed(seed)
    .iterations(iterations)
    .optimizationAlgo(OptimizationAlgorithm.LINE_GRADIENT_DESCENT)
```

To a create a ListBuilder with the specified layers (here it is eight), we call the `.list()` method:

```
.list(8)
```

The next step now is to build the encoding phase of the model. This can be done by the subsequent addition of the Restricted Boltzmann machine into the model. The encoding phase has four layers of the restricted Boltzmann machine in which each layer would have `2000`, `1000`, `500`, and `30` nodes respectively:

```
.layer(0, new RBM.Builder().nIn(numRows *
numColumns).nOut(2000).lossFunction(LossFunctions.LossFunction
.RMSE_XENT).build())
.layer(1, new RBM.Builder().nIn(2000).nOut(1000)
.lossFunction(LossFunctions.LossFunction.RMSE_XENT).build())
.layer(2, new RBM.Builder().nIn(1000).nOut(500)
.lossFunction(LossFunctions.LossFunction.RMSE_XENT).build())
.layer(3, new RBM.Builder().nIn(500).nOut(30)
.lossFunction(LossFunctions.LossFunction.RMSE_XENT).build())
```

The next phase after encoder is the decoder phase, where we will use four more Restricted Boltzmann machines in a similar manner:

```
.layer(4, new RBM.Builder().nIn(30).nOut(500)
.lossFunction(LossFunctions.LossFunction.RMSE_XENT).build())
.layer(5, new RBM.Builder().nIn(500).nOut(1000)
.lossFunction(LossFunctions.LossFunction.RMSE_XENT).build())
.layer(6, new RBM.Builder().nIn(1000).nOut(2000)
.lossFunction(LossFunctions.LossFunction.RMSE_XENT).build())
.layer(7, new OutputLayer.Builder(LossFunctions.LossFunction.MSE)
.activation("sigmoid").nIn(2000).nOut(numRows*numColumns).build())
```

As all the intermediate layers are now built, we can build the model by calling the `build()` method:

```
.pretrain(true).backprop(true)
.build();
```

The last phase of the implementation is to train the deep autoencoder. It can be done by calling the `fit ()` method:

```
MultiLayerNetwork model = new MultiLayerNetwork(conf);
model.init();

model.setListeners(new ScoreIterationListener(listenerFreq));

log.info("Train model....");
while(iter.hasNext())
  {
    DataSet next = iter.next();
    model.fit(new DataSet(next.getFeatureMatrix(),next
    .getFeatureMatrix()));
  }
```

Denoising autoencoder

The reconstruction of output from input does not always guarantee the desired output, and can sometimes end up in simply copying the input. To prevent such a situation, in [134], a different strategy has been proposed. In that proposed architecture, rather than putting some constraints in the representation of the input data, the reconstruction criteria is built, based on cleaning the partially corrupted input.

> *"A good representation is one that can be obtained robustly from a corrupted input and that will be useful for recovering the corresponding clean input."*

A denoising autoencoder is a type of autoencoder which takes corrupted data as input, and the model is trained to predict the original, clean, and uncorrupted data as its output. In this section, we will explain the basic idea behind designing a denoising autoencoder.

Architecture of a Denoising autoencoder

The primary idea behind a denoising autoencoder is to introduce a corruption process, $Q (k' \mid k)$, and reconstruct the output r from the corrupted input k'. *Figure 6.6* shows the overall representation of a denoising autoencoder. In a denoising autoencoder, for every minibatch of training data k, the corresponding corrupted k' should be generated using $Q (k' \mid k)$. From there, if we consider the initial input as the corrupted input k', then the whole model can be considered as a form of a basic encoder. The corrupted input k' is mapped to generate the hidden representation h.

Therefore, we get the following:

$$h = f(k') = Wk' + b$$

From this hidden representation, the reconstructed output, *r*, can be derived using $r = g\ (h)$. Denoising autoencoder reorganizes the data, and then tries to learn about the data for the reconstruction of the output. This reorganization of the data or shuffling of the data generates the noise, and the model learns the features from the noise, which allows categorizing the input. During training of the network, it produces a model, which computes the distance between that model and the benchmark through a loss function. The idea is to minimize the average reconstruction error over a training set to make the output r as close as possible to the original uncorrupted input *k*.

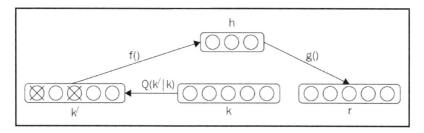

Figure 6.6: The steps involved in designing a denoising autoencoder. The original input is k; corrupted input derived from k is denoted as k'. The final output is denoted as r.

Stacked denoising autoencoders

The basic concept of building a stacked denoising autoencoder to initialize a deep neural network is similar to stacking a number of Restricted Boltzmann machines to build a Deep Belief network or a traditional deep autoencoder. The generation of corrupted input is only needed for the initial denoising training of each of the individual layers to help in learning the useful features extraction.

Once we know the encoding function *f* to reach the hidden state, it is used on the original, uncorrupted data to reach the next level. In general, no corruption or noise is put to generate the representation, which will act as an uncorrupted input for training the next layer. A key function of a stacked denoising autoencoder is its layer-by-layer unsupervised pre-training as the input is fed through. Once a layer is pre-trained to perform the feature selection and extraction on the input from the preceding layer, the next stages of supervised fine tuning can follow, just as in case of the traditional deep autoencoders.

Figure 6.7 shows the detailed representation to design a stacked denoising autoencoder. The overall procedure for learning and stacking multiple layers of a denoising autoencoder is shown in the following figure:

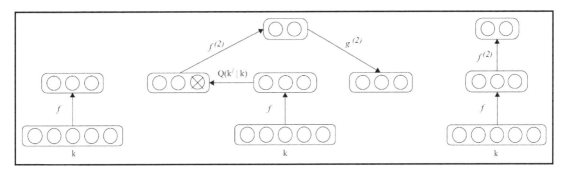

Figure 6.7: The representation of a stacked denoising autoencoder

Implementation of a stacked denoising autoencoder using Deeplearning4j

Stacked denoising autoencoders can be built using Deeplearning4j by creating a `MultiLayerNetwork` that possesses autoencoders as its hidden layers. The autoencoders have some `corruptionLevel`, which is denoted as noise.

Here we set the initial configuration needed to set up the model. For illustration purposes, a `batchSize` of `1024` numbers of examples is taken. The input number and output number is taken as `1000` and `2` respectively.

```
int outputNum = 2;
int inputNum = 1000;
int iterations = 10;
int seed = 123;
int batchSize = 1024;
```

The loading of the input dataset is the same as explained in the deep autoencoder section. Therefore, we will directly jump to how to build the stack denoising autoencoder. We have taken a five-hidden-layer deep model to illustrate the method:

```
log.info ("Build model....");
MultiLayerConfiguration conf = new NeuralNetConfiguration.Builder ()
  .seed(seed)
  .gradientNormalization(GradientNormalization
  .ClipElementWiseAbsoluteValue)
```

```
.gradientNormalizationThreshold (1.0)
.iterations(iterations)
.updater(Updater.NESTEROVS)
.momentum(0.5)
.momentumAfter(Collections.singletonMap(3, 0.9))
.optimizationAlgo(OptimizationAlgorithm.CONJUGATE_GRADIENT)
.list()
.layer(0, new AutoEncoder.Builder()
  .nIn(inputNum)
  .nOut(500)
  .weightInit(WeightInit.XAVIER).lossFunction(LossFunction.RMSE_XENT)
```

The following code denotes how much input data is to be corrupted:

```
.corruptionLevel (0.3)
.build())
.layer(1, new AutoEncoder.Builder()
  .nIn(500)
  .nOut(250)
  .weightInit(WeightInit.XAVIER).lossFunction
  (LossFunction.RMSE_XENT)
  .corruptionLevel(0.3)
  .build())
.layer(2, new AutoEncoder.Builder()
  .nIn(250)
  .nOut(125)
  .weightInit(WeightInit.XAVIER).lossFunction
  (LossFunction.RMSE_XENT)
  .corruptionLevel(0.3)
  .build())
.layer(3, new AutoEncoder.Builder()
  .nIn(125)
  .nOut(50)
  .weightInit(WeightInit.XAVIER).lossFunction
  (LossFunction.RMSE_XENT)
  .corruptionLevel(0.3)
  .build())
.layer(4, new OutputLayer.Builder
(LossFunction.NEGATIVELOGLIKELIHOOD)
  .activation("softmax")
  .nIn(75)
  .nOut(outputNum)
  .build())
.pretrain(true)
.backprop(false)
.build();
```

Once the model is built, it is trained by calling the `fit()` method:

```
try {
    model.fit(iter);
    }
catch(Exception ex)
    {
    ex.printStackTrace();
    }
```

Applications of autoencoders

Autoencoders can be successfully applied in many use cases, and hence, have gained much popularity in the world of deep learning. In this section, we will discuss the important applications and uses of autoencoders:

- **Dimensionality reduction**: If you remember, in `Chapter 1`, *Introduction to Deep Learning*, we introduced the concept of the 'curse of dimensionality'. Dimensionality reduction was one of the first applications of deep learning. Autoencoders were initially studied to overcome the issues with the curse of dimensionality. We have already got a fair idea from this chapter how deep autoencoders work on higher-dimensional data to reduce the dimensionality in the final output.

- **Information Retrieval**: One more important application of autoencoders is in information retrieval. Information retrieval basically means to search for some entries, which match with an entered query, in a database. Searching in high-dimensional data is generally a cumbersome task; however, with reduced dimensionality of a dataset, the search can become extremely efficient in certain kinds of lower dimensional data. The dimensionality reduction obtained from the autoencoder can generate codes that are low dimensional and binary in nature. These can be stored in a key values stored data structure, where keys are binary code vectors and values are the corresponding entries. Such key value stores help us to perform information retrieval by returning all the database entries that match some binary code with the query. This approach to retrieving information through dimensionality reduction and binary code is called semantic hashing [135].

- **Image Search**: As explained in the deep autoencoder section, deep autoencoders are capable of compressing image datasets of higher dimensions to a very small number of vectors, say 30. Therefore, this has made image searching easier for high-dimensional images. Once an image is uploaded, the search engine will compress it into small vectors, and then compare that vector to all the others in its index. For a search query, the vectors that contain similar numbers will be returned and translated into the mapped image.

Summary

Autoencoders, one of the most popular and widely applicable generative models, have been discussed in this chapter. Autoencoders basically help two phases: one is the encoder phase and the other is the decoder phase. In this chapter, we elaborated on both of these phases with suitable mathematical explanations. Going forward, we explained a special kind of autoencoder called the sparse autoencoder. We also discussed how autoencoders can be used in the world of deep neural networks by explaining deep autoencoders. Deep autoencoders consist of layers of Restricted Boltzmann machines, which take part in the encoder and decoder phases of the network. We explained how to deploy deep autoencoders using Deeplearning4j, by loading chunks of the input dataset into a Hadoop Distributed File System. Later in this chapter, we introduced the most popular form of autoencoder called the denoising autoencoder and its deep network version known as the stacked denoising autoencoder. The implementation of a stacked denoising autoencoder using Deeplearning4j was also shown. We concluded this chapter by outlining the common applications of autoencoders.

In the next chapter, we will discuss some common useful applications of deep learning with the help of Hadoop.

7

Miscellaneous Deep Learning Operations using Hadoop

"In pioneer days they used oxen for heavy pulling, and when one ox couldn't budge a log, they didn't try to grow a larger ox. We shouldn't be trying for bigger computers, but for more systems of computers."

— Grace Hopper

So far in this book, we discussed various deep neural network models and their concepts, applications, and implementation of the models in distributed environments. We have also explained why it is difficult for a centralized computer to store and process vast amounts of data and extract information using these models. Hadoop has been used to overcome the limitations caused by large-scale data.

As we have now reached the final chapter of this book, we will mainly discuss the design of the three most commonly used machine learning applications. We will explain the general concept of large-scale video processing, large-scale image processing, and natural language processing using the Hadoop framework.

The organization of this chapter is as follows:

- Large-scale distributed video processing using Hadoop
- Large-scale image processing using Hadoop
- Natural language processing using Hadoop

The large amount of videos available in the digital world are contributing to the lion's share of the big data generated in recent days. In `Chapter 2`, *Distributed Deep Learning for Large-Scale Data* we discussed how millions of videos are uploaded to various social media websites such as YouTube and Facebook. Apart from this, surveillance cameras installed for security purposes in various shopping malls, airports, or government organizations generate loads of videos on a daily basis. Most of these videos are typically stored as compressed video files due to their huge storage consumption. In most of these enterprises, the security cameras operate for the whole day and later store the important videos, to be investigated in future.

These videos contain hidden "hot data" or information, which needs to be processed and extracted quickly. As a consequence, the need to process and analyze these large-scale videos has become one of the priorities for data enthusiasts. Also, in many different fields of studies, such as bio-medical engineering, geology, and educational research, there is a need to process these large-scale videos and make them available at different locations for detailed analysis.

In this section, we will look into the processing of large-scale video datasets using the Hadoop framework. The primary challenge of large-scale video processing is to transcode the videos from compressed to uncompressed format. For this reason, we need a distributed video transcoder that will write the video in the **Hadoop Distributed File System** (**HDFS**), decode the bit stream chunks in parallel, and generate a sequence file.

When a block of the input data is processed in the HDFS, each mapper process accesses the lines in each split separately. However, in case of a large-scale video dataset, when it is split into multiple blocks of predefined sizes, each mapper process is supposed to interpret the blocks of bit-stream separately. The mapper process will then provide access to the decoded video frames for subsequent analysis. In the following subsections, we will discuss how each block of the HDFS containing the video bit-stream can be transcoded into sets of images to be processed for the further analyses.

Distributed video decoding in Hadoop

Most of the popular video compression formats, such as MPEG-2 and MPEG-4, follow a hierarchical structure in the bit-stream. In this subsection, we will assume that the compression format used has a hierarchical structure for its bit-stream. For simplicity, we have divided the decoding task into two different Map-reduce jobs:

1. **Extraction of video sequence level information**: From the outset, it can be easily predicted that the header information of all the video dataset can be found in the first block of the dataset. In this phase, the aim of the map-reduce job is to collect the sequence level information from the first block of the video dataset and output the result as a text file in the HDFS. The sequence header information is needed to set the format for the decoder object.

For the video files, a new `FileInputFormat` should be implemented with its own record reader. Each record reader will then provide a `<key, value>` pair in this format to each map process: `<LongWritable, BytesWritable>`. The input key denotes the byte offset within the file; the value that corresponds to `BytesWritable` is a byte array containing the video bit-stream for the whole block of data.

For each map process, the key value is compared with `0` to identify if it is the first block of the video file. Once the first block is identified, the bit-stream is parsed to determine the sequence level information. This information is then dumped to a `.txt` file to be written to HDFS. Let's denote the name of the `.txt` file as `input_filename_sequence_level_header_information.txt`. As only the map process can provide us the desired output, the reducer count for this method is set to `0`.

Assume a text file with the following data:
Deep Learning
with Hadoop
Now the offset for the first line is `0` and the input to the Hadoop job will be `<0, Deep Learning>` and for the second line the offset will be `<14, with Hadoop>`.
Whenever we pass the text file to the Hadoop job, it internally calculates the byte offset.

2. **Decode and convert the blocks of videos into sequence files**: The aim of this Map-reduce job is to decode each block of the video datasets and generate a corresponding sequence file. The sequence file will contain the decoded video frames of each block of data in JPEG format. The `InputFileFormat` file and record reader should be kept same as the first Map-reduce job. Therefore, the `<key, value>` pairs of the mapper input is `<LongWritable, BytesWritable>`.

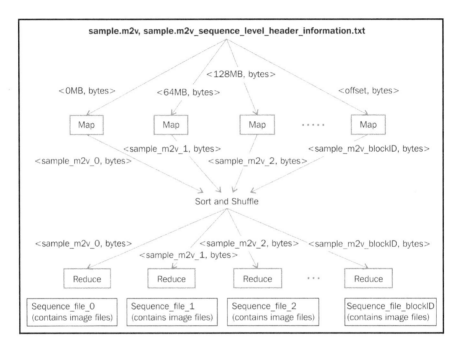

Figure 7.1: The overall representation of video decoding with Hadoop

- In this second phase, the output of the first job is considered as the input to this second Map-reduce job. Therefore, each mapper of this job will read the sequence information file in the HDFS and pass this information along with the bit-stream buffer, which comes as the `BytesWritable` input.

- The map process basically converts the decoded video frames to JPEG images and generates a `<key, value>` pair as the output of the map process. The key of this output of the map process encodes the input video filename and the block number as `video_filename_block_number`. The output value that corresponds to this key is `BytesWritable`, and it stores the JPEG bit-stream of the decoded video block.

- The reducers will then take the blocks of data as input and simply write the decoded frames into a sequence file containing JPEG images as output format for further processing. A simple format and overview of the whole process is shown in *Figure 7.1*. We have taken an input video `sample.m2v` for illustration purposes. Further, in this chapter, we will discuss how to process the large-scale image files (from the sequence files) with the HDFS.

Input `<key,value>` for Mapper: `<LongWritable, BytesWritable>`

For example: `<17308965, BytesWritable>`

Output `<key,value>` from Mapper: `<Text, BytesWritable>`

For example: `<sample.m2v_3, BytesWritable>`

Large-scale image processing using Hadoop

We have already mentioned in the earlier chapters how the size and volume of images are increasing day by day; the need to store and process these vast amount of images is difficult for centralized computers. Let's consider an example to get a practical idea of such situations. Let's take a large-scale image of size 81025 pixels by 86273 pixels. Each pixel is composed of three values: red, green, and blue. Consider that, to store each of these values, a 32-bit precision floating point number is required. Therefore, the total memory consumption of that image can be calculated as follows:

$$86273 * 81025 * 3 * 32 \ bits = 78.12 \ GB$$

Leave aside doing any post processing on this image, as it can be clearly concluded that it is impossible for a traditional computer to even store this amount of data in its main memory. Even though some advanced computers come with higher configurations, given the return on investment, most companies do not opt for these computers as they are much too expensive to be acquired and maintained. Therefore, the proper solution should be to run the images in commodity hardware so that the images can be stored in their memory. In this section, we will explain the use of Hadoop to process these vast amounts of images in a distributed manner.

Application of Map-Reduce jobs

In this section, we will discuss how to process large image files using Map-reduce jobs with Hadoop. Before the job starts, all the input images to be processed are loaded to the HDFS. During the operation, the client sends a job request, which goes through NameNode. NameNode collects that request from the client, searches its metadata mapping, and then sends the data block information of the filesystem as well as location of the data block back to the client. Once the client gets the block's metadata, it automatically accesses the DataNodes, where the requested data block resides, then processes this data via the applicable commands.

The Map-reduce jobs used for large-scale image processing are primarily responsible for controlling the whole task. Basically, here we explain the concept of an executable shell script file, which is responsible for collecting the executable file's input data from the HDFS.

The best way to use the Map-reduce programming model is to design our own Hadoop data types for processing large numbers of image files directly. The system will use Hadoop Streaming technology, which helps the users to create and run special kinds of Map-reduce jobs. These special kinds of jobs can be performed through an executable file mentioned earlier, which will act as a mapper or reducer. The mapper implementation of the program will use a shell script to perform the necessary operation. The shell script is responsible for calling the executable files of the image processing. The lists of image files are taken as the input to these executable files for further processing. The results of this processing or output are later written back to the HDFS.

So, the input image files should be written to the HDFS first, and then a file list is generated in a particular directory of Hadoop Streaming's input. The directory will store a collection of file lists. Each line of the file list will contain the HDFS address of the images files to be processed. The input of the mapper will be `Inputsplit` class, which is a text file. The shell script manager reads the files line by line and retrieves the images from the metadata. It then calls the image processing executable file for further processing of the images, and then write the result back to the HDFS. Hence, the output of the mapper is the final desired result. The mapper thus does all the jobs, retrieving the image file from the HDFS, image processing, and then writing it back to the HDFS. The number of reducers in this process can be set to zero.

This is a simple design of how to process large numbers of images using Hadoop by the binary image processing method. Other complex image processing methods can also be deployed to process large-scale image datasets.

Natural language processing using Hadoop

The exponential growth of information in the Web has increased the intensity of diffusion of large-scale unstructured natural language textual resources. Hence, in the last few years, the interest to extract, process, and share this information has increased substantially. Processing these sources of knowledge within a stipulated time frame has turned out to be a major challenge for various research and commercial industries. In this section, we will describe the process used to crawl the web documents, discover the information and run natural language processing in a distributed manner using Hadoop.

To design architecture for **natural language processing** (**NLP**), the first task to be performed is the extraction of annotated keywords and key phrases from the large-scale unstructured data. To perform the NLP on a distributed architecture, the Apache Hadoop framework can be chosen for its efficient and scalable solution, and also to improve the failure handling and data integrity. The large-scale web crawler can be set to extract all the unstructured data from the Web and write it in the Hadoop Distributed File System for further processing. To perform the particular NLP tasks, we can use the open source GATE application as shown in the paper [136]. An overview of the tentative design of a distributed natural language processing architecture is shown in *Figure 7.2*.

To distribute the working of the web crawler, map-reduce can be used and run across multiple nodes. The execution of the NLP tasks and also the writing of the final output is performed with Map-reduce. The whole architecture will depend on two input files i) the `seedurls` given for crawling a particular web page stored in `seed_urls.txt` and ii) the path location of the NLP application (such as where GATE is installed). The web crawler will take `seedurls` from the `.txt` file and run the crawler for those in parallel. Asynchronously, an extraction plugin searches the keywords and key phrases on the crawled web pages and executes independently along with the web pages crawled. At the last step, a dedicated program stores the extracted keywords and key phrases in an external SQL database or a NoSQL database such as `Elasticsearch`, as per the requirements. All these modules mentioned in the architecture are described in the following subsections.

Web crawler

To explain this phase, we won't go into a deep explanation, as it's almost out of the scope of this book. Web crawling has a few different phases. The first phase is the URL discovery stage, where the process takes each seed URL as the input of the `seed_urls.txt` file and navigates through the pagination URLs to discover relevant URLs. This phase defines the set of URLs that are going to be fetched in the next phase.

The next phase is fetching the page content of the URLs and saving in the disk. The operation is done segment-wise, where each segment will contain some predefined numbers of URLs. The operation will run in parallel on different `DataNodes`. The final outcome of the phases is stored in the Hadoop Distributed File System. The Keyword extractor will work on these saved page contents for the next phase.

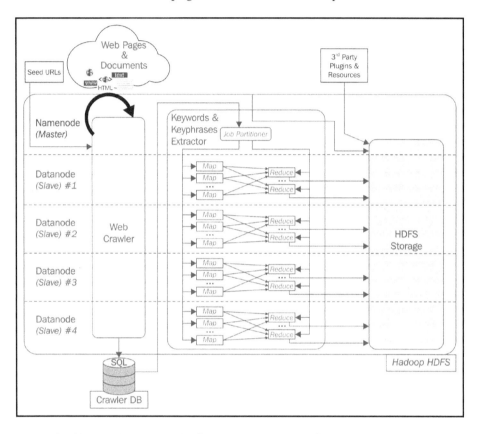

Figure 7.2: The representation of how natural language processing is performed in Hadoop that is going to be fetched in the next phase. The next phase is fetching the page content of the URLs and saving in the disk. The operation is done segment wise, where each segment will contain some pre-defined numbers of URLs. The operation will run in parallel on different DataNodes. The final outcome of the phases is stored in Hadoop Distributed File System. The keyword extractor will work on these saved page contents for the next phase.

Extraction of keyword and module for natural language processing

For the page content of each URL, a **Document Object Model** (**DOM**) is created and stored back in the HDFS. In the *DOM*, documents have a logical structure like a tree. Using DOM, one can write the `xpath` to collect the required keywords and phrases in the natural language processing phase. In this module, we will define the Map-reduce job for executing the natural language processing application for the next phase. The map function defined as a `<key, value>` pair key is the URL, and values are a corresponding DOM of the URL. The *reduce* function will perform the configuration and execution of the natural language processing part. The subsequent estimation of the extracted keywords and phrases at the web domain level will be performed in the `reduce` method. For this purpose, we can write a custom plugin to generate the rule files to perform various string manipulations to filter out the noisy, undesired words from the extracted texts. The rule files can be a JSON file or any other easy to load and interpret file based on the use case. Preferably, the common nouns and adjectives are identified as common keywords from the texts.

Estimation of relevant keywords from a page

The paper [136] has presented a very important formulation to find the relevant keywords and key phrases from a web document. They have provided the **Term Frequency – Inverse Document Frequency** (**TF-IDF**) metric to estimate the relevant information from the whole corpus, composed of all the documents and pages that belong to a single web domain. Computing the value of *TD-IDF* and assigning it a threshold value for discarding other keywords allows us to generate the most relevant words from the corpus. In other words, it discards the common articles and conjunctions that might have a high frequency of occurrence in the text, but generally do not possess any meaningful information. The *TF-IDF* metric is basically the product of two functions, *TF* and *IDF*.

TF provides the frequency of each word in the corpus, that is, how many times a word is present in the corpus. Whereas *IDF* behaves as a balance term, showing higher values for terms having the lower frequency in the whole corpus.

Mathematically, the metric *TF-IDF* for a keyword or key phrase *i* in a document *d* contained in the document *D* is given by the following equation:

$$(TF\text{-}IDF)_i = TF_i \cdot IDF_i$$

Here $TF_i = f_i/n_d$ and $IDF_i = log\ N_d/N_i$

Here f_i is the frequency of the candidate keyword or key phrase i in the document d and n_d is the total number of terms in the document d. In *IDF*, N_D denotes the total number of documents present in the corpus D, whereas N_i denotes the number of documents in which the keyword or key phrase i is present.

Based on the use cases, one should define a generic threshold frequency for *TF-IDF*. For a keyword or key phrase i if the value of *TF-IDF* becomes higher than the threshold value, that keyword or key phrase is accepted as final as written directly to the HDFS. On the other hand, if the corresponding value is less than the threshold value, that keyword is dropped from the final collection. In that way, finally, all the desired keywords will be written to the HDFS.

Summary

This chapter discussed the most widely used applications of Machine learning and how they can be designed in the Hadoop framework. First, we started with a large video set and showed how the video can be decoded in the HDFS and later converted into a sequence file containing images for later processing. Large-scale image processing was discussed next in the chapter. The mapper used for this purpose has a shell script which performs all the tasks necessary. So, no reducer is necessary to perform this operation. Finally, we discussed how the natural language processing model can be deployed in Hadoop.

References

[1] Hsu, F.-H. (2002). Behind Deep Blue: Building the Computer That Defeated the World Chess Champion . Princeton University Press, Princeton, NJ, USA.

[2] Geoffrey E. Hinton, Simon Osindero, and Yee-Whye Teh. 2006. A fast learning algorithm for deep belief nets. Neural Comput. 18, 7 (July 2006), 1527-1554.

[3] Bengio, Yoshua, et al. "Greedy layer-wise training of deep networks." Advances in neural information processing systems 19 (2007): 153.

[4] Krizhevsky, Alex, Ilya Sutskever, and Geoffrey E. Hinton. "Imagenet classification with deep convolutional neural networks." Advances in neural information processing systems. 2012.

[5] Machine Learning, Tom Mitchell, McGraw Hill, 1997.

[6] Machine Learning: A Probabilistic Perspective (Adaptive Computation and Machine Learning series), Kevin P. Murphy

[7] O. Chapelle, B. Scholkopf and A. Zien Eds., "Semi-Supervised Learning (Chapelle, O. et al., Eds.; 2006) [Book reviews]," in IEEE Transactions on Neural Networks, vol. 20, no. 3, pp. 542-542, March 2009.

[8] Y. Bengio. Learning deep architectures for AI. in Foundations and Trends in Machine Learning, 2(1):1–127, 2009.

[9] G. Dahl, D. Yu, L. Deng, and A. Acero. Context-dependent DBNHMMs in large vocabulary continuous speech recognition. In Proceedings of International Conference on Acoustics Speech and Signal Processing (ICASSP). 2011.

[10] A. Mohamed, G. Dahl, and G. Hinton. Acoustic modeling using deep belief networks. IEEE Transactions on Audio, Speech, & Language Processing, 20(1), January 2012.

[11] A. Mohamed, D. Yu, and L. Deng. Investigation of full-sequence training of deep belief networks for speech recognition. In Proceedings of Inter speech. 2010.

[12] Indyk, Piotr, and Rajeev Motwani. "Approximate nearest neighbors: towards removing the curse of dimensionality." Proceedings of the thirtieth annual ACM symposium on Theory of computing. ACM, 1998.

[13] Friedman, Jerome H. "On bias, variance, 0/1—loss, and the curse-of-dimensionality." Data mining and knowledge discovery 1.1 (1997): 55-77.

[14] Keogh, Eamonn, and Abdullah Mueen. "Curse of dimensionality." Encyclopedia of Machine Learning. Springer US, 2011. 257-258.

[15] Hughes, G.F. (January 1968). "On the mean accuracy of statistical pattern recognizers". IEEE Transactions on Information Theory. 14 (1): 55–63.

[16] Bengio, Yoshua, Patrice Simard, and Paolo Frasconi. "Learning long-term dependencies with gradient descent is difficult." IEEE transactions on neural networks 5.2 (1994): 157-166.

[17] Ivakhnenko, Alexey (1965). Cybernetic Predicting Devices. Kiev: Naukova Dumka.

[18] Ivakhnenko, Alexey (1971). "Polynomial theory of complex systems". IEEE Transactions on Systems, Man and Cybernetics (4): 364–378.

[19] X. Glorot and Y. Bengio. Understanding the difficulty of training deep feed-forward neural networks. In Proceedings of Artificial Intelligence and Statistics (AISTATS). 2010.

[20] G. Hinton and R. Salakhutdinov. Reducing the dimensionality of data with neural networks. Science, 313(5786):504–507, July 2006

[21] M. Ranzato, C. Poultney, S. Chopra, and Y. LeCun. Efficient learning of sparse representations with an energy-based model. In Proceedings of Neural Information Processing Systems (NIPS). 2006.

[22] I. Goodfellow, M. Mirza, A. Courville, and Y. Bengio. Multi-prediction deep boltzmann machines. In Proceedings of Neural Information Processing Systems (NIPS). 2013.

[23] R. Salakhutdinov and G. Hinton. Deep boltzmann machines. In Proceedings of Artificial Intelligence and Statistics (AISTATS). 2009.

[24] R. Salakhutdinov and G. Hinton. A better way to pretrain deep boltzmann machines. In Proceedings of Neural Information Processing Systems (NIPS). 2012.

[25] N. Srivastava and R. Salakhutdinov. Multimodal learning with deep boltzmann machines. In Proceedings of Neural Information Processing Systems (NIPS). 2012.

[26] H. Poon and P. Domingos. Sum-product networks: A new deep architecture. In Proceedings of Uncertainty in Artificial Intelligence. 2011.

[27] R. Gens and P. Domingo. Discriminative learning of sum-product networks. Neural Information Processing Systems (NIPS), 2012.

[28] R. Gens and P. Domingo. Discriminative learning of sum-product networks. Neural Information Processing Systems (NIPS), 2012.

[29] S. Hochreiter. Untersuchungen zu dynamischen neuronalen netzen. Diploma thesis, Institut fur Informatik, Technische Universitat Munchen, 1991.

[30] J.Martens. Deep learning with hessian-free optimization. In Proceedings of international Conference on Machine Learning (ICML). 2010.

[31] Y. Bengio. Deep learning of representations: Looking forward. In Statistical Language and Speech Processing, pages 1–37. Springer, 2013.

[32] I. Sutskever. Training recurrent neural networks. Ph.D. Thesis, University of Toronto, 2013.

[33] J. Ngiam, Z. Chen, P. Koh, and A. Ng. Learning deep energy models. In Proceedings of International Conference on Machine Learning (ICML). 2011.

[34] Y. LeCun, S. Chopra, M. Ranzato, and F. Huang. Energy-based models in document recognition and computer vision. In Proceedings of International Conference on Document Analysis and Recognition (ICDAR). 2007.

[35] R. Chengalvarayan and L. Deng. Speech trajectory discrimination using the minimum classification error learning. IEEE Transactions on Speech and Audio Processing, 6(6):505–515, 1998.

[36] M. Gibson and T. Hain. Error approximation and minimum phone error acoustic model estimation. IEEE Transactions on Audio, Speech, and Language Processing, 18(6):1269–1279, August 2010

[37] X. He, L. Deng, andW. Chou. Discriminative learning in sequential pattern recognition — a unifying review for optimization-oriented speech recognition. IEEE Signal Processing Magazine, 25:14–36, 2008.

[38] H. Jiang and X. Li. Parameter estimation of statistical models using convex optimization: An advanced method of discriminative training for speech and language processing. IEEE Signal Processing Magazine, 27(3):115–127, 2010.

[39] B.-H. Juang, W. Chou, and C.-H. Lee. Minimum classification error rate methods for speech recognition. IEEE Transactions On Speech and Audio Processing, 5:257–265, 1997.

[40] D. Povey and P. Woodland. Minimum phone error and I-smoothing for improved discriminative training. In Proceedings of International Conference on Acoustics Speech and Signal Processing (ICASSP). 2002

[41] D. Yu, L. Deng, X. He, and X. Acero. Large-margin minimum classification error training for large-scale speech recognition tasks. In Proceedings of International Conference on Acoustics Speech and Signal Processing (ICASSP). 2007.

[42] A. Robinson. An application of recurrent nets to phone probability estimation. IEEE Transactions on Neural Networks, 5:298–305, 1994

[43] A. Graves. Sequence transduction with recurrent neural networks. Representation Learning Workshop, International Conference on Machine Learning (ICML), 2012.

[44] A. Graves, S. Fernandez, F. Gomez, and J. Schmidhuber. Connectionist temporal classification: Labeling unsegmented sequence data with recurrent neural networks. In Proceedings of International Conference on Machine Learning (ICML). 2006.

[45] A. Graves, N. Jaitly, and A. Mohamed. Hybrid speech recognition with deep bidirectional LSTM. In Proceedings of the Automatic Speech Recognition and Understanding Workshop (ASRU). 2013.

[46] A. Graves, A. Mohamed, and G. Hinton. Speech recognition with deep recurrent neural networks. In Proceedings of International Conference on Acoustics Speech and Signal Processing (ICASSP). 2013

[47] K. Lang, A. Waibel, and G. Hinton. A time-delay neural network architecture for isolated word recognition. Neural Networks, 3(1):23–43, 1990.

[48] A.Waibel, T. Hanazawa, G. Hinton, K. Shikano, and K. Lang. Phoneme recognition using time-delay neural networks. IEEE Transactions on Acoustical Speech, and Signal Processing, 37:328–339, 1989.

[50] Moore, Gordon E. (1965-04-19). "Cramming more components onto integrated circuits". Electronics. Retrieved 2016-07-01.

[51] http://www.emc.com/collateral/analyst-reports/idc-the-digital-universe-in-2020.pdf

[52] D. Beaver, S. Kumar, H. C. Li, J. Sobel, and P. Vajgel, \Finding a needle in haystack: Facebooks photo storage," in OSDI, 2010, pp. 4760.

[53] Michele Banko and Eric Brill. 2001. Scaling to very very large corpora for natural language disambiguation. In Proceedings of the 39th Annual Meeting on Association for Computational Linguistics (ACL '01). Association for Computational Linguistics, Stroudsburg, PA, USA, 26-33.

[54] http://www.huffingtonpost.in/entry/big-data-and-deep-learnin_b_3325352

[55] X. W. Chen and X. Lin, "Big Data Deep Learning: Challenges and Perspectives," in IEEE Access, vol. 2, no. , pp. 514-525, 2014.

[56] Bengio Y, LeCun Y (2007) Scaling learning algorithms towards, AI. In: Bottou L, Chapelle O, DeCoste D, Weston J

(eds). Large Scale Kernel Machines. MIT Press, Cambridge, MA Vol. 34. pp 321–360. http://www.iro.umontreal.ca/~lisa/pointeurs/bengio+lecun_chapter2007.pdf

[57] A. Coats, B. Huval, T. Wng, D. Wu, and A. Wu, "Deep Learning with COTS HPS systems," J. Mach. Learn. Res., vol. 28, no. 3, pp. 1337-1345, 2013.

[58] J.Wang and X. Shen, "Large margin semi-supervised learning," J. Mach. Learn. Res., vol. 8, no. 8, pp. 1867-1891, 2007

[59] R. Fergus, Y. Weiss, and A. Torralba, "Semi-supervised learning in gigantic image collections," in Proc. Adv. NIPS, 2009, pp. 522-530.

[60] J. Ngiam, A. Khosla, M. Kim, J. Nam, H. Lee, and A. Ng, "Multimodal deep learning," in Proc. 28th Int. Conf. Mach. Learn., Bellevue, WA, USA, 2011

[61] N. Srivastava and R. Salakhutdinov, "Multimodal learning with deep Boltzmann machines," in Proc. Adv. NIPS, 2012

[62] L. Bottou, "Online algorithms and stochastic approximations," in On-Line Learning in Neural Networks, D. Saad, Ed. Cambridge, U.K.: Cambridge Univ. Press, 1998.

[63] A. Blum and C. Burch, "On-line learning and the metrical task system problem," in Proc. 10th Annu. Conf. Comput. Learn. Theory, 1997, pp. 45-53.

[64] N. Cesa-Bianchi, Y. Freund, D. Helmbold, and M. Warmuth, "On-line prediction and conversation strategies," in Proc. Conf. Comput. Learn. Theory Eurocolt, vol. 53. Oxford, U.K., 1994, pp. 205-216.

[65] Y. Freund and R. Schapire, "Game theory, on-line prediction and boosting," in Proc. 9th Annu. Conf. Comput. Learn. Theory, 1996, pp. 325-332.

[66] Q. Le et al., "Building high-level features using large scale unsupervised learning," in Proc. Int. Conf. Mach. Learn., 2012.

[67] C. P. Lim and R. F. Harrison, "Online pattern classifcation with multiple neural network systems: An experimental study," IEEE Trans. Syst., Man, Cybern. C, Appl. Rev., vol. 33, no. 2, pp. 235-247, May 2003.

[68] P. Riegler and M. Biehl, "On-line backpropagation in two-layered neural networks," J. Phys. A, vol. 28, no. 20, pp. L507-L513, 1995

[69] M. Rattray and D. Saad, "Globally optimal on-line learning rules for multi-layer neural networks," J. Phys. A, Math. General, vol. 30, no. 22, pp. L771-776, 1997.

[70] P. Campolucci, A. Uncini, F. Piazza, and B. Rao, "On-line learning algorithms for locally recurrent neural networks," IEEE Trans. Neural Netw., vol. 10, no. 2, pp. 253-271, Mar. 1999

[71] N. Liang, G. Huang, P. Saratchandran, and N. Sundararajan, "A fast and accurate online sequential learning algorithm for feedforward networks," IEEE Trans. Neural Netw., vol. 17, no. 6, pp. 1411-1423, Nov. 2006.

[72] L. Bottou and O. Bousequet, "Stochastic gradient learning in neural networks," in Proc. Neuro-Nimes, 1991.

[73] S. Shalev-Shwartz, Y. Singer, and N. Srebro, "Pegasos: Primal estimated sub-gradient solver for SVM," in Proc. Int. Conf. Mach. Learn., 2007.

[74] D. Scherer, A. Müller, and S. Behnke, "Evaluation of pooling operations in convolutional architectures for object recognition," in Proc. Int. Conf. Artif. Neural Netw., 2010, pp. 92-101.

[75] J. Chien and H. Hsieh, "Nonstationary source separation using sequential and variational Bayesian learning," IEEE Trans. Neural Netw. Learn. Syst., vol. 24, no. 5, pp. 681-694, May 2013.

[76] W. de Oliveira, "The Rosenblatt Bayesian algorithm learning in a nonstationary environment," IEEE Trans. Neural Netw., vol. 18, no. 2, pp. 584-588, Mar. 2007.

[77] Hadoop Distributed File System, http://hadoop.apache.org/2012.

[78] T. White. 2009. Hadoop: The Definitive Guide. OReilly Media, Inc. June 2009

[79] Shvachko, K.; Hairong Kuang; Radia, S.; Chansler, R., May 2010. The Hadoop Distributed File System,"2010 IEEE 26th Symposium on Mass Storage Systems and Technologies (MSST). vol., no., pp.1,10

[80] Hadoop Distributed File System, https://hadoop.apache.org/docs/stable/hadoop-project-dist/hadoop-hdfs/.

[81] Dev, Dipayan, and Ripon Patgiri. "Dr. Hadoop: an infinite scalable metadata management for Hadoop—How the baby elephant becomes immortal." Frontiers of Information Technology & Electronic Engineering 17 (2016): 15-31.

[82] http://deeplearning4j.org/

[83] Dean, Jeffrey, and Sanjay Ghemawat. "MapReduce: simplified data processing on large clusters." Communications of the ACM 51.1 (2008): 107-113.

[84] http://deeplearning.net/software/theano/

[85] http://torch.ch/

[86] Borthakur, Dhruba. "The hadoop distributed file system: Architecture and design." Hadoop Project Website 11.2007 (2007): 21.

[87] Borthakur, Dhruba. "HDFS architecture guide." HADOOP APACHE PROJECT https://hadoop.apache.org/docs/r1.2.1/hdfs_design.pdf(2008): 39.

[88] http://deeplearning4j.org/quickstart

[89] LeCun, Yann, and Yoshua Bengio. "Convolutional networks for images, speech, and time series." The handbook of brain theory and neural networks 3361.10 (1995): 1995.

[90] LeCun, Y., Bottou, L., Bengio, Y., and Haffner, P. (1998). Gradient-based learning applied to document recognition. Proc. IEEE 86, 2278–2324. doi:10.1109/5.726791

[91] Gao, H., Mao, J., Zhou, J., Huang, Z., Wang, L., and Xu, W. (2015). Are you talking to a machine? Dataset and methods for multilingual image question answering. arXiv preprint arXiv:1505.05612.

[92] Srinivas, Suraj, et al. "A Taxonomy of Deep Convolutional Neural Nets for Computer Vision." arXiv preprint arXiv:1601.06615 (2016).

[93] Zhou, Y-T., et al. "Image restoration using a neural network." IEEE Transactions on Acoustics, Speech, and Signal Processing 36.7 (1988): 1141-1151.

[94] Maas, Andrew L., Awni Y. Hannun, and Andrew Y. Ng. "Rectifier nonlinearities improve neural network acoustic models." Proc. ICML. Vol. 30. No. 1. 2013.

[95] He, Kaiming, et al. "Delving deep into rectifiers: Surpassing human-level performance on imagenet classification." Proceedings of the IEEE International Conference on Computer Vision. 2015.

[96] http://web.engr.illinois.edu/~slazebni/spring14/lec24_cnn.pdf

[97] Zeiler, Matthew D., and Rob Fergus. "Visualizing and understanding convolutional networks." European Conference on Computer Vision. Springer International Publishing, 2014.

[98] Simonyan, Karen, and Andrew Zisserman. "Very deep convolutional networks for large-scale image recognition." arXiv preprint arXiv:1409.1556 (2014).

[99] Szegedy, Christian, et al. "Going deeper with convolutions." Proceedings of the IEEE Conference on Computer Vision and Pattern Recognition. 2015.

[100] He, Kaiming, et al. "Deep residual learning for image recognition." arXiv preprint arXiv:1512.03385 (2015).

[101] Krizhevsky, Alex. "One weird trick for parallelizing convolutional neural networks." arXiv preprint arXiv:1404.5997 (2014).

[102] S. Hochreiter and J. Schmidhuber. Long short-term memory. Neural computation, 9(8):1735–1780, 1997.

[103] Mikolov, Tomas, et al. "Recurrent neural network based language model." Interspeech. Vol. 2. 2010.

[104] Rumelhart, D. E., Hinton, G. E., and Williams, R. J. (1986). Learning representations by backpropagating errors. Nature, 323, 533–536.

[105] Mikolov, T., Sutskever, I., Chen, K., Corrado, G., and Dean, J. (2013a). Distributed representations of words and phrases and their compositionality. In Advances in Neural Information Processing Systems 26, pages 3111–3119.

[106]Graves, A. (2013). Generating sequences with recurrent neural networks. arXiv:1308.0850 [cs.NE].

[107] Pascanu, R., Mikolov, T., and Bengio, Y. (2013a). On the difficulty of training recurrent neural networks. In ICML'2013.

[108] Mikolov, T., Sutskever, I., Deoras, A., Le, H., Kombrink, S., and Cernocky, J. (2012a). Subword language modeling with neural networks. unpublished

[109] Graves, A., Mohamed, A., and Hinton, G. (2013). Speech recognition with deep recurrent neural networks. ICASSP

[110] Graves, A., Liwicki, M., Fernandez, S., Bertolami, R., Bunke, H., and Schmidhuber, J. (2009). A novel connectionist system for improved unconstrained handwriting recognition. IEEE Transactions on Pattern Analysis and Machine Intelligence.

[111] http://karpathy.github.io/2015/05/21/rnn-effectiveness/

[112] https://web.stanford.edu/group/pdplab/pdphandbook/handbookch8.html

[113] Schuster, Mike, and Kuldip K. Paliwal. "Bidirectional recurrent neural networks." IEEE Transactions on Signal Processing 45.11 (1997): 2673-2681.

[114] Graves, Alan, Navdeep Jaitly, and Abdel-rahman Mohamed. "Hybrid speech recognition with deep bidirectional LSTM." Automatic Speech Recognition and Understanding (ASRU), 2013 IEEE Workshop on. IEEE, 2013

[115] Baldi, Pierre, et al. "Exploiting the past and the future in protein secondary structure prediction." Bioinformatics 15.11 (1999): 937-946

[116] Hochreiter, Sepp, and Jürgen Schmidhuber. "Long short-term memory." Neural computation 9.8 (1997): 1735-1780.

[117] A. Graves, M. Liwicki, S. Fernandez, R. Bertolami, H. Bunke, J. Schmidhuber. A Novel Connectionist System for Improved Unconstrained Handwriting Recognition. IEEE Transactions on Pattern Analysis and Machine Intelligence, vol. 31, no. 5, 2009.

[118] With QuickType, Apple wants to do more than guess your next text. It wants to give you an AI.". WIRED. Retrieved 2016-06-16

[119] Sak, Hasim, Andrew W. Senior, and Françoise Beaufays. "Long short-term memory recurrent neural network architectures for large scale acoustic modeling." INTERSPEECH. 2014.

[120] Poultney, Christopher, Sumit Chopra, and Yann L. Cun. "Efficient learning of sparse representations with an energy-based model." Advances in neural information processing systems. 2006.

[121] LeCun, Yann, et al. "A tutorial on energy-based learning." Predicting structured data 1 (2006): 0.

[122] Ackley, David H., Geoffrey E. Hinton, and Terrence J. Sejnowski. "A learning algorithm for Boltzmann machines." Cognitive science 9.1 (1985): 147-169.

[123] Desjardins, G. and Bengio, Y. (2008). Empirical evaluation of convolutional RBMs for vision. Technical Report 1327, Département d'Informatique et de Recherche Opérationnelle, Université de Montréal.

[124] Hinton, G. E., Osindero, S., and Teh, Y. (2006). A fast learning algorithm for deep belief nets. Neural Computation, 18, 1527–1554.

[125] Hinton, G. E. (2007b). Learning multiple layers of representation. Trends in cognitive sciences , 11(10), 428–434.

[126] Bengio, Yoshua, et al. "Greedy layer-wise training of deep networks." Advances in neural information processing systems 19 (2007): 153.

[127] A.-R. Mohamed, T. N. Sainath, G. Dahl, B. Ramabhadran, G. E. Hinton, and M. A. Picheny, "Deep belief networks using discriminative features for phone recognition," in Proc. IEEE ICASSP, May 2011, pp. 5060-5063.

[128] R. Salakhutdinov and G. Hinton, "Semantic hashing," Int. J. Approx. Reasoning, vol. 50, no. 7, pp. 969-978, 2009.

[129] G. W. Taylor, G. E. Hinton, and S. T. Roweis, "Modeling human motion using binary latent variables," in Advances in Neural Information Processing Systems. Cambridge, MA, USA: MIT Press, 2006, pp. 1345-1352.

[130] Zhang, Kunlei, and Xue-Wen Chen. "Large-scale deep belief nets with mapreduce." IEEE Access 2 (2014): 395-403.

[131] Yoshua Bengio, Aaron Courville, and Pascal Vincent. Representation learning: A review and new perspectives. Technical report, arXiv:1206.5538, 2012b.

[132] Makhzani, Alireza, and Brendan Frey. "k-Sparse Autoencoders." arXiv preprint arXiv:1312.5663 (2013).

[133] Hinton, Geoffrey E., and Ruslan R. Salakhutdinov. "Reducing the dimensionality of data with neural networks." Science 313.5786 (2006): 504-507.

[134] Vincent, Pascal, et al. "Stacked denoising autoencoders: Learning useful representations in a deep network with a local denoising criterion." Journal of Machine Learning Research 11.Dec (2010): 3371-3408.

[135] Salakhutdinov, Ruslan, and Geoffrey Hinton. "Semantic hashing." RBM 500.3 (2007): 500.

[136] Nesi, Paolo, Gianni Pantaleo, and Gianmarco Sanesi. "A hadoop based platform for natural language processing of web pages and documents." Journal of Visual Languages & Computing 31 (2015): 130-138.

Index

www.ingramcontent.com/pod-product-compliance
Lightning Source LLC
LaVergne TN
LVHW081341050326
832903LV00024B/1255